BURY MY
HEART IN
BERMONDSEY

Also by Barry Albin Dyer

Don't Drop the Coffin
Strong Shoulders
Final Departures

BURY MY HEART IN BERMONDSEY

Barry Albin Dyer

Hodder & Stoughton
LONDON SYDNEY AUCKLAND

First published in Great Britain in 2004
This paperback edition first published in 2006

The right of Barry Albin Dyer to be identified as the Author of
the Work has been asserted by him in accordance with
the Copyright, Designs and Patents Act 1988.

1

British Library Cataloguing in Publication Data
A record for this book is available from the British Library

ISBN 0 340 90918 8

Typeset in Goudy by Avon DataSet Ltd,
Bidford-on-Avon, Warwickshire

Printed and bound in Great Britain by
Clays Ltd, St Ives plc

The paper and board used in this paperback are natural recyclable
products made from wood grown in sustainable forests.
The manufacturing processes conform to the environmental
regulations of the country of origin.

Hodder & Stoughton
A Division of Hodder Headline Ltd
338 Euston Road
London NW1 3BH
www.madaboutbooks.com

CONTENTS

To the bereaved; there is always hope (and if my books make a difference, I am very privileged).

To those who fight to hang on to this life daily – be strong as you are ambassadors of courage.

To the wonderful people of Bermondsey and Rotherhithe, now encompassed by the Borough of Southwark. Your courage and spirit lives on, and as always you inspire me!

And to my Mum, Mary Angela Dyer, who died with cancer when I was seventeen years old. I will always love you, Mum, even though you made me wear idiot mittens at school!

A sum from the net royalties of this book will be paid
to two charities that mean a lot to me. First is the Albin-Dyer
Bermondsey & Rotherhithe Foundation, my own local charity
set up to assist local people, clubs, churches, other charities
and foundations, but most of all local families in need.
Second is the Evelina Children's Hospital, which has
cared for thousands of local children over many years.
As a child, they nursed me through illness and operations.
The year 2004 will see the opening of their new building
at St Thomas' Hospital, in South East London,
and long may they continue their good work.

ACKNOWLEDGEMENTS

Many thanks go to the following for their help with the writing of this book:

The National Society of Allied Independent Funeral Directors (SAIF), and the National Association of Funeral Directors.

Pharos; *Longevity Reports*; *The Immortalist*; *Funeral Services Journal*; *Thanos* (published by FIAT/IFTA); *The Funeral Director*; *The Journal*; and many other trade journals.

All the wonderful staff at Albins, and the many dedicated staff who work so hard in every funeral directors businesses in the British Isles – you are great people. Thank you for every experience and every story that I have been able to share.

'Bermondsey', a local history of the borough.

The Internet(!)

Terence Dinan, for the wonderful Bermondsey poem.

And last but never least, my family.

Bermondsey, My Bermondsey

Bermondsey, my Bermondsey, never out of my mind.
A place on the map one can easily find.
Where are the houses, the folk that I knew?
The streets have all changed, and the faces are new.

Remember Dockhead? And Father Murnane?
A priest whom no one e'er turned to in vain.
A man for the people, in church or at court.
He lived for his parish, for his parish he fought.

The Catholic Procession – what an annual event!
Those streets lined with people, and many knees bent.
The hymns and the floats, the lorries and vans.
The noise and the hush, the prayers and the bands.

Those Orpington boys, their pillbox on head.
Their drum and fife band, the tears that were shed.
Those bright sturdy lads, orphans each and every one.
Touched the hearts of us all, our feelings were wrung.

The Downside and Fisher, remember those clubs?
Kept lads off the streets and out of the pubs.
The pursuit was sport, and all played the game.
Danny Lynch and some others, achieved national fame.

Father Stephen who sponsored and founded both clubs.
And Freddie Kirkpatrick who reined in the subs.
The war changed it all, and many are gone.
The rest are old men, but club spirit lives on.

Remember the cinemas, 'The Storks' and 'The Star'?
A side door conveniently left on the jar.
One crept up the stairs and bided one's time,
Then mixed with the crowd. Who'd call it a crime?

Remember the pubs – 'The Hole in the Wall',
'The Stingo' and 'Feathers', 'The Moonies' and all?
And old 'Muttoneye' wedged in the door of a bar,
With harmonium he'd carried, goodness knows from how far!

Bermondsey, Bermondsey, we were all of us poor.
No violence, no muggings, we kept to the law.
The neighbours so close, and the people so kind.
Those faces and places, never fade from my mind.

Part of a poem dedicated to Canon Arbuthnott
by Terence Dinan

The epitome of my passion for Bermondsey – my first and last
home.

PREFACE

How much time do we all spend worrying about things that will probably never happen or promising to do things that we probably should do but never will? As human beings, we instinctively need to worry. Should we constantly plan our lives and the lives of those around us, or should we just let what will be, be? We also naturally, and sometimes unnaturally, spend a considerable amount of time worrying about death and dying, yet the truth is that whenever death comes, it will always be at the end of life. So the question is only one of timing. Best then that we think about this for a moment, understand that it exists, acknowledge it and move on to enjoy life, because for all its troubles our real purpose here is to live it the best way we can.

From our first breath, we are learning to live, often by instinct but mostly from the people around us. If being a funeral director has taught me anything, it is to understand the value of each moment and each other. Health and love! We are all constantly facing death; it is always with us. For some, it is an impending enemy that they are courageously facing now, and these amazing people have been included in the dedication to this book.

As I finished the last chapter of *Final Departures*, my second book, I told myself that I would never write another book. As always, true to myself, here it is! So what changed my mind? Well, I had written two books, the first of which, *Don't Drop the Coffin*, was then republished with extra photos and work from the television series. The television series itself was just finishing, and the response from the public for more of both the television series and my books was truly and completely overwhelming. But one very special letter among thousands convinced me that I could make a difference by my writing. My book was not a great literary work of art but just me talking about much of my knowledge, thoughts and, I hope, humour out loud. And as I always say, laughter and tears are the same emotion.

But what of the letter that changed my mind? It came from one of the very people included in the dedication in the sincere hope that they will overcome death as an immediate adversary and send it way back to where it belongs – at the end of their life – or, if that is just not possible, overcome it by confronting it with peace and love, accepting that, in that way, its fear can also be defeated. We are all afraid of death, but it is part of life that we must all transcend.

The letter itself came from a very brave person who had undergone treatment for cancer, had truly had enough and was about to give up. That person watched the television series and went on to read my book; both gave them the hope and courage enough to try again. That person is still fighting and holding their own with their life-and-death struggle. Whatever the final outcome, I am assured that this person faces death now with less fear and enjoys every precious moment that life offers them. Everyone in this position has my support, respect and admiration.

If you have read either of my books, you will know how I fight an ongoing battle with bereavement and pain. I will continue to campaign to help the bereaved in the long journey surrounding the dreadful illness that is bereavement. I sincerely hope that by writing about my life, stories both funny and sad, we may all understand the stigma of death a little better.

God Bless.

Barry Albin Dyer

FOREWORD BY PETER HINDLEY

As many people know, Barry was born in Bermondsey; educated in Bermondsey, grew up into the family business in Bermondsey and is now a local character in Bermondsey. I, however, was born in central Africa, the son of a medical missionary, was educated in an English public school and started my career in the upmarket store of Harrods.

I now count Barry as one of my personal friends, and you may well ask yourself the question 'How on earth can oil and water mix?'! But there is far more to it than this: Barry has a very successful family funeral business and I am Chief Executive of the country's largest funeral services provider.

I got to know Barry some fifteen years ago, and as I started talking to him, we both realised that although we came from very different backgrounds and we ran very different businesses, there were many things that we could learn from each other. The skills and strengths that I require to run a large organisation are, for instance, very different from those which Barry requires to run his family business. As an example, Barry knows each one of his staff very personally and has breakfast with all of them most mornings. I have over two thousand staff spread around the country from Scotland down to Cornwall, and therefore my method of communication with and motivation of my staff is very different from the very hands-on approach that Barry can have. It is in these very different ways that Barry and I have come to respect each other's abilities and skills, and to learn from each other in a very special way.

I visit Barry's business on a regular basis, where he is very open to showing me the things that he is doing, and we share experiences. Barry also provides me with a good thermometer on how my business in London is doing, as he is constantly out on funerals and in crematoria at the same time as my staff, and he clearly observes what is going on.

Because of our relationship, we have been able to create a joint-venture company that handles the international repatriation of deceased. Barry's involvement in international matters has helped the development of this organisation; this, together with the facilities that my company can provide, made a great combination, and the business goes from strength to strength.

We have also been able to pool our resources and help each other when it comes to the purchase of some of our funeral requirements. Because we need large quantities of certain items, Barry has had the contacts abroad to introduce us to suppliers so that we can negotiate keen terms, and Barry has been able to benefit by taking advantage of the prices that we have been able to negotiate.

The purpose of going into this detail is to demonstrate that there are huge benefits from the relationship that Barry and I have, both from a business point of view and personally, and although we come from very different backgrounds and experiences, we are able to be friends and business colleagues, appreciating and learning from our 'differences'.

I am sure that you will thoroughly enjoy reading this book and I wish Barry well for its successful launch.

Peter Hindley

FOREWORD BY STEPHEN JOEL

I first discovered Barry Dyer whilst lolling in a morning bath. Barry was appearing on my old mate Danny Baker's breakfast show on BBC London – little did I know that a chance twiddle of the tuning dial on my radio would start what turned into a remarkable experience. Within just one year of that radio broadcast, six episodes of *Don't Drop the Coffin* had been researched, filmed, edited and transmitted on ITV1, to critical acclaim.

My television career to this point had been spent 'having a bit of a laugh', producing programmes such as *TFI Friday*, *Beadle's About* and *Don't Forget Your Toothbrush* amongst others, but now I was camped out for four months at F.A. Albin & Sons Funeral Directors, Bermondsey. Showbiz? Well, yes. Every funeral has a bit of showbiz about it, as every family in their own way wants to send off their lost loved ones in the best way they feel fit. And there is no better place for them to do this than at Barry's remarkable firm, in the safe, compassionate and understanding hands of his staff.

I had never set foot in an undertakers before my first meeting with Barry and was expecting to meet a dour, Dickens-like Mr Sowerbury figure; how wrong I was. Also, I had been to only a handful of funerals in my life, and those had all been cremations. I was blown away by the place, the people and the way they went about their daily business. I was hooked, and I think our five million viewers were hooked too. Four months later, filming was finished. Myself and the rest of the production team packed away our cameras and went back to Soho's media land with its trendy bars and its 'beautiful people', but we sure miss the welcome that we received every morning from the twenty-eight or so staff at F.A. Albin & Sons. Genuine people doing a genuine job, every one of them. I take my hat off to them all.

Stephen Joel

BEORMUND'SEY ~ PAST AND PRESENT

Bermondsey began well over a thousand years ago as a small island, probably named after an early Anglo-Saxon lord, Beormund, who owned the land. This island, Beormund'sey, was a low piece of land slightly raised out above the marshy ground and surrounding streams. Much of Bermondsey as we know it today lies below the level of the River Thames, and about two thousand years ago, well before its existence, the Romans built a wall to protect the area from the river water.

Its first real recognition came in the Doomsday Book of 1086, with a mention of Bermondsey Abbey, famous as one of the country's greatest religious monasteries. Even from early days, the people of Bermondsey were known as close-knit and 'stayers', often living their whole lives in the one small area, working and frequently existing in bad conditions. All that is left from the old Abbey days is the parish church of St Mary Magdalene, now the oldest building left standing in Bermondsey, boasting well over a hundred thousand baptisms, of which I was one!

Many people believe that where we are born is a matter of fate. For me, however, it is far more than that. I regard myself as lucky to have been born in Bermondsey, living my life and working here – but why is anybody born anywhere? In my own case, it was very simple: being near to my mum seemed to be a good idea – and very important to her at the time. But other exceptional people, both past and present, have in some way been associated with Bermondsey, Southwark and Rotherhithe. And many more, of course, have yet to be born.

I would have to write another book to mention all the amazing people who have been born here, lived here, worked here or in some other way contributed to the area, but I have picked just a few to mention. Overwhelmingly, however, the real backbone in this area is made up of the everyday people, like myself, my family and so many of my local friends and clients. In themselves and as a group, they are its real strength. Like all communities we lack many things, but what we have never lacked, will never lack and can never lack is character. Bermondsey folk are the most friendly I have ever come across, even though to the outside world they may sometimes seem a little fearsome. The most commonly used phrase in Bermondsey is, 'Can I help you, mate?' Bermondsey, Rotherhithe, Southwark – as we are all labelled today – is just the best.

So, in no particular order whatsoever, I give you:

William Shakespeare, actor and world-renowned writer
Charlie Chaplin, music hall entertainer and film star
Max Bygraves, entertainer and singer
Bob Mellish, one of Bermondsey's longest serving and finest
    MPs

Prince Lee Boo, famous Prince of Belau (an island in the South China Sea), who is buried in St Mary's Church, Rotherhithe

The Pilgrim Fathers, who set sail on the *Mayflower* from Rotherhithe to Plymouth en route to find a new world

Dr Alfred Salter, local doctor and MP

Tommy Steele, born Tommy Hicks, an entertainer and film star

Major Bevington, who gave employment to so many people from Bermondsey and was a great supporter of local education

Samuel Pepys, famous for his diaries

Sir Michael Caine, born Michael Micklewhite, the world-famous actor

Michael Faraday, inventor and one of the developers of electricity through the creation of generators and transformers

Simon Hughes, another of the longest serving, and certainly hardest working, local MPs

Charles Dickens, one of the world's greatest authors, who like so many people in Bermondsey used the experiences of his own life to create some wonderful characters and stories.

Southwark has also been home to many sporting heroes, war heroes and inventors, and has certainly had its share of incredible, even notorious, people. It is a place where so much has happened and so much will undoubtedly continue to happen, I am sure of that.

For example, at Spa Road was one of the first stations in London and one of the country's first fresh spring-water spas. The area gave a home to great ship-builders and the first dog-biscuit factory in the UK. The first abbey in London was in

Bermondsey, and in the 1880s the Royal Surrey Zoological Gardens in Walworth were filled with lions, tigers, elephants and giraffes, a first for London.

Many famous foods have been produced here: Sarson's vinegar, Courage ale, Jacob's biscuits, Edward's doughnuts, Peak Frean's biscuits, Hartley's jams, Crosse & Blackwell soups and other products, and Pearce Duff's custard. Walworth also had a wonderful fruit and vegetable garden – peaches, grapes and all kinds of exotic produce.

The area has been home to great rope-makers, as well as being a centre for the tanning and leather industry, with a wonderful leather market. Connected with this, Bermondsey was famous for making superb shoes, which is why we have here the church of St Crispin, the patron saint of leather and shoe-makers. Bermondsey is also home to the Caledonian Antiques Market, one of the oldest and most famous antiques markets of our time.

I could go on and on, but this is just to whet your appetite for the wonderful and colourful history of my birthplace. You can uncover new finds all the time. In fact, I only recently found out that Rotherhithe Street is not just one of the oldest streets in London but definitely the longest.

As well as being noted for our history and manufacturing, we have developed our own vocabulary: 'oojamaflip' (for when you can't think of the name of something), 'whatchamacallit' (again for when you can't think of the name of something), 'thingymebob' (also for when you can't think of the name of something) and 'wotsitsname' (yes, you've guessed it – for when you can't think of the name of something). We really are an inventive lot!

The many sayings and phrases of Cockney rhyming slang would again need a whole book to contain them, and I am

sure somebody has already logged them. Here are just a few
that are commonly used in South London:

Pie and liquor	Vicar
Apples and pears	Stairs
Hasn't got a Scooby Doo	Hasn't got a clue
Oi Oi Saveloy	To get your attention (my granddaughter Olivia's favourite)
Tin tack	The sack
Dicky dirt	Shirt
Callard & Bowsers	Trousers
Daisy roots	Boots
Rhythm and blues	Shoes
Whistle and flute	Suit
Harry Lime	Time
Sky rocket	Pocket
Kettle and hob	Fob (watch)
Billy Fury	Jury
Saucepan lid	Kid
Franny Lees	Keys
Custard and jelly	Telly
Roger Moore	Door
Carving knife	Wife
Haddock and bloater	Motor
Bent as a nine bob note	Somebody who is not straight with you
Lovely jubbly	Great stuff
Jack Jones	On your own

People say Bermondsey has changed. Correct; of course it's
changed - it's changed since the day it existed. There is
nothing wrong with change. Without it, I guess, the human

race would probably no longer exist. And we are all guilty of looking back and remembering only the good old times, never the bad, while still truly knowing that today will be the good old times for our children. There is no right or wrong in this.

For me, my childhood in Bermondsey was always full of smells. Smells that stay with me today in my memory and sometimes even still fill the air. Down Weston Street next to Guy's Hospital, where I was born, there was a smell of pepper from Arker's, the pepper factory. Walk a little further along and you would be in Leathermarket Street, with the amazing smell of the tannery, and the vinegar from the Sarson's factory. Through into Bermondsey Street and there was a mixture of smells of spices, bread baking from the large bakery and, on a Friday morning at the bottom of Bermondsey Street, the Caledonian Market, with sounds and smells of all kinds. Along Grange Walk, late Horney Lane, there would be a dreadful smell from the fur factory (very unpleasant, I always used to think). Round into Spa Road to the wonderful Spa Bakery – fresh bread, cakes, doughnuts. Aah, wonderful whiffs. A few doors along to Frank's Fish Shop, with its unmistakable smell on a late evening – fish and chips and a penny's worth of crackling. Smashing! A little bit further along Spa Road there was the Pearce and Duff's custard factory, turning out all nature of fresh, sweet smells. Around into Grange Road and you would have the smell of the perfume factory; that was always vile, goodness knows why. As much as I like perfume, that was nothing like perfume! Through down the Blue with the stalls – fruit, vegetables, meat, fish, you name it – it was wonderful. Then the baking days from Peak Frean's at the bottom of the Blue in Drummond Road. Every day of the week had a different smell as they baked a different biscuit: coconut, shortbread, my mouth is watering just thinking about it. Then Armand Road, by the arches where Albin's kept their cars for so many years and which was so much a part of my youth; there was the brilliant smell of chocolate from the forward-thinking Shuttleworth's factory.

I could go on and on, I honestly could. Characters, real life people too many to mention. Bermondsey was, and still is, full of them. For me, the finest people I have ever met in Bermondsey are my dad and Fred Albin, who have been a lifetime's inspiration to me. May they live forever; they certainly will in my heart. But although many of Bermondsey's characters have changed and many, or most, of the old smells have gone, the spirit lives on and the old smells have been replaced with new ones.

Today, as I walk along Rotherhithe Street and past the Mogul Indian restaurant, there is the spicy smell of my Friday night curry, home delivered to the door; who could ask for more? Down Jamaica Road and past the new Pizza Castello, with its wonderful smell of fresh pizzas. Back down Spa Road and we still have the fish and chip shop, no crackling now though sadly - not good for the cholesterol, of course. And still the Spa Bakery, under new management but still full of lovely aromas. Down to the Borough Market on a Saturday morning where the air is thick with the smell of fresh coffee, fruit and vegetables. The hustle and bustle of people. Scented candles. All manner of smells. These will be the smells that our kids grow up remembering. And finally to my favourite Bermondsey restaurant at Dockhead, Saturday night special at La Lanterna - fabulous.

Many of the houses are no longer there, and many of the horizons have gone or changed. Some homes have been replaced with luxury apartments and riverside houses, and we now have what I think is a beautiful view of Canary Tower and the surrounding buildings. But through all this, the heart of Bermondsey still beats. There are of course the usual inner city problems of crime and grime, but for every unsavoury thing Bermondsey remains shining like a diamond in a jamboree bag. Full of diamond geezers. People who are the dogs (as they say). Yes, we know we have a bit of tunnel vision. We don't want the Euro; I mean, how would we describe our money if it were no longer a jacks for a fiver, a cockle for a tenner, a score for a twenty, a pony for twenty-five or a bullseye for fifty, a ton for a hundred, a monkey for five hundred and a grand for a thousand? As our favourite unsung hero Del Boy from television's *Only Fools and Horses* would say, 'In Bermondsey we are *millionaires*, Rodney.'

It might be nice to live somewhere else for a while. It's nice to get away for a holiday, although coming back is always really special for me. For some people, it is better to move away; for others, better to stay. I make no judgements about where or how people choose to live their lives. It is interesting though that many people who move out of Bermondsey, rarely moving too far, usually into places like Sidcup, Bexley, Eltham, Chistlehurst, areas just on the borders of Kent, often find themselves back in Bermondsey having a drink in a local pub, perhaps visiting a relative or continuing to support their local football club, Millwall, Fisher, whatever it may be. It is also really interesting how many of those people come back to Bermondsey to Albin's when they have a death in the family. I have so much respect for all of them, I really do.

Bermondsey people are often criticised for seeing things their own way, but, come on, who doesn't? There are problems in Bermondsey, just as there are problems everywhere, but there is a warmth that still exists today which is almost impossible to put into words. Perhaps it is just something that runs through your veins, but, whatever it is, to say it's special is an understatement.

For some time now, I have had a great interest in the story of the American Indian. I was lucky enough, with my family, to visit the American Indian Museum in New York, down in Harlem. The trip was a fantastic eye-opener and taught me so much about the American Indians and the passion and sacredness of the land they lived upon – or, more accurately, were once at one with. This then led me to read a book called *Bury My Heart at Wounded Knee*, the true story of the American Indian (thanks to my very special pal Paul Darnell). Perhaps the one thing the American Indian, even the American Indian of today, and I have in common is a sacred belief in and love for the place of our birth.

It was with this in mind and with the encouragement of my publishers, in particular Charles and David, that I chose to name this, my third book, *Bury My Heart in Bermondsey*. I make no apologies for being sloppy and sentimental about Bermondsey. I believe we live our lives in rings of three: the past, the present and the future. My past and my present are entwined with Bermondsey and I see no reason why my future, or even my death, should be any different.

When reading my books, you cannot escape realising how much I love and admire the area in which I live and the people I share it with.

Many things have continued to change but 'Beormund'sey' is still here. And so is its spirit. Look in on us if you're passing – we don't bite! And if I should die in Bermondsey, think only this of me: leave me there!

1

PASSION

People say that it is sad to die penniless, but I think it could really be perfect. Imagine just spending your last penny on whatever convenience it might be for whatever reason, and then exhaling your last breath. Some might say this would be the perfect end to the perfect life.

Others, however, would disagree and say that there are no pockets in a shroud, although they could always be sewn in, I suppose, and history would witness thousands of people – like the pharaohs of ancient Egypt – who did take it with them contrary to common belief that you cannot. There are those, of course, like my cryonic suspension friends, who believe that they will return to this life at a later date, putting their money in trusts in places like Liechtenstein, protected and safe until they return. Who can say whether those funds will just sit there until the end of time? Others try to rule from the grave with wills that extend themselves into the lives of those they leave behind, commanding them to live in a certain fashion if they want to inherit. But, given the choice, none of us really wants to live on through what we have achieved in this life – we all truly want to extend the life we already have. So where does death fit into the stages of life, or is it just an extension of life itself? Complicated, isn't it – or is it?

When we get right down to it, I think it is really very simple. At the beginning of our lives, we are just an extension of our mothers, and it takes us as children time to realise that we are people in our own right. From that moment on, anything in our lives is possible, anything can happen. Life can be short, long, rise in huge plateaux, fall to great depressions. There may be moments of despair, moments of great joy. Some of us may simply plod on in straight lines on an uneventful path. However we look at it, though, life is an event in itself and death the greatest mystery in that event. So in truth, the only really certain thing about life is that death will occur. It is just a matter of timing.

For me, the greatest gift we can be given or achieve after that of life itself is passion. If you have true passion, how can you fail? Take the great football manager Alex Ferguson – not that I'm a Manchester United fan, of course (Millwall and Liverpool for me!) – but is there a more passionate manager anywhere or a more passionate person in himself? What would he have on his gravestone, do you think? Probably, 'I would sooner be here than at Man City'.

Bernard Manning, a man with a huge passion for both comedy and Manchester City, once said, 'When they had burglars at Manchester City who broke into the trophy room and pinched the lot, the police put out a call saying that they were looking for a man with a roll of blue carpet under his arm.' Being able to laugh like this at your own passion is also really important. Bernard has made a very good living through being able to laugh at himself and everything around him. I heard him say that he is now a very wealthy man but was once very poor. 'In fact,' he said, 'when I was a kid we used to sleep six in a bed, and five of them constantly wet themselves. I learned to swim before I could walk, and when my dad used to ask where I wanted to sleep, I'd say, "The shallow end, if you please."'

The passion that often confronts you as a funeral director is, however, of a very different nature, and I can only admire people who have the courage to speak up at such a terrible time in their lives, making their feelings and their wishes clear to everybody. That's not an easy thing to do.

A recent experience with a family I know quite well is a brilliant example of such courage. Charlie was a popular local businessman whom I had known in the area for a number of years. In his sixties, he was a nice, small-framed gentleman – very dapper as we say here in Bermondsey (that's very smartly dressed, of course). Now Charlie had had his life tragically taken from him while working at his business yard. Somebody had been lying in wait for him and, as he was about to leave his car, shot him in cold blood. Nobody can really say why this happened, but as far as I know the person who did it has never been caught. You can only imagine that it must have been some kind of contract killing, but does violence of that kind ever solve anything? Doesn't it merely hurt everybody who's left around that person, innocent people who truly loved him? Violence is never the answer. Sure, Charlie had been a ducker and a diver, but God knows why this should have happened at this stage of his life.

As is the procedure in the UK, it took some time for the coroner to release Charlie's body to us. We did everything we could to make him viewable for his family and back to his old, dapper self. His family brought in his favourite clothes and chose a very special coffin for him, and he was laid to rest in our chapel here in Culling Road in Bermondsey so that the family could come and go as they wished. On this particular day, a Bank Holiday, I had agreed to open up the business so that the family could come together and spend a couple of hours with Charlie. Charlie had a huge family – children, grandchildren, great-grandchildren – and he loved them all very much. He had been the centre of their life. They all arrived promptly and went in to sit with him, talk to him, talk about his life to each other. It was really lovely. I arranged tea and coffee for them, and they came in and out, sitting in the lounge area we have at the front, chatting to me and then going back in to see Charlie. Every so often, somebody would pop out, having thought of something for the day of the funeral, to check with me whether we had arranged this or that request. The funeral itself was planned to be a very lovely occasion, an absolute tribute to his life by his family. They were to have floral cars, endless limousines, horses and a fantastic service that was to include gospel singers and some brilliant tributes from his friends, who had shared with him a traditional upbringing from childhood. Many of them belonged, as Charlie did, to the local boxing club – the Fisher Downside Worth Club – one of the most famous boxing clubs in the country, which has furnished many a world champion. The tributes to Charlie's life were to be very special.

As the family finally, one by one, said goodbye on that Bank Holiday Monday, they left the chapel and congregated just outside. It was a quiet, sunny day, and I noticed that there was deep conversation going on between several of the family. Then Charlie's wife called me over. The granddaughter was, I noticed, in floods of tears, almost inconsolable, and her grandmother was saying to her, 'Well, darling, if we have him home it's going to be very difficult for us, and he is well looked after here.'

Then she turned to me and said, 'Barry knew Grandad, he'll look after him.'

At that point, the granddaughter turned to me and screamed in my face, 'You didn't know my grandad, you don't. Nanny, don't leave him here with these people. Don't leave him. You didn't know my grandad. You didn't, did you? Nan, he's got to come home with us. He's got to be with us, not here with these people, please, please. You didn't know my grandad.'

Her nan immediately turned and apologised: 'I am so sorry, Barry.'

I quickly replied, 'No! Please don't be sorry. Darling, I knew your grandad but not like you knew him, not as family, and I truly admire your passion. I think it's absolutely wonderful that you have the courage and the intention to speak like this. She's right – I knew him, but I didn't know him like any of you, and it's you that he is really, really special to. But darling, I'll care for him in exactly the same way as you would, and you can come and see him whenever you really feel you have to, OK? You just lift the phone and I'll be here. But please don't apologise, because your passion is fantastic and I admire you enormously, all of you.'

The whole family seemed to be settled and consoled by this, and agreed that they would go home and talk about it further. In the end, they were happy for Charlie to spend his last few days here with us before he left for his funeral. This is just an example of how important passion is; when it is involved in bereavement it can be angry passion, but it is still right. You have to see through what a person is saying to what he or she is actually feeling inside. That's how important the job of a funeral director is, because if you cannot see through those words, into the heart and see that passion, you should not be doing that job. If your heart's empty, what's in your head doesn't really matter. Or, to put it another way, if you don't like everybody, how can you help anybody?

I will never forget that young girl's courage. She led the way at a most difficult time, and her family, although a little embarrassed (unnecessarily, I have to say), loved her dearly. That love and warmth could be felt around everything that was going on that day. The family felt that this should not have been Charlie's time, and they were quite rightly feeling very cheated by life itself.

Another local man I knew well over the years, Eddie, expressed a passion of a different kind even in death. Eddie died suddenly of a heart attack, and when I found out the full circumstances of the life he lived, I have to say I am not surprised he went this way. Eddie was a very loveable character in more ways than one, and it was certainly not just his friends and family who loved him, because Eddie was a bit of a ladies' man too! Although Eddie was married with a family of grown-up girls and boys, and even though he was in his fifties, he had certainly not lost any of his passion for the fair sex.

I was standing at the front of the church assisting Father Patrick with the thurible – the brass cup on a chain containing hot charcoal and incense that allows the spirit to rise to Heaven in peace through the smoke – and found myself wondering just how Eddie had been able to keep it all up. You can take that any way you like, because sitting in the second and third rows were six women he was currently involved with. Six! That took me aback too, but it is quite true, I promise you! Apparently Eddie had been like this all through his life. In some way or other, his wife had been able to accept this as a failing that she could not change. Not that she did not care, but she loved him in every other way and just accepted the situation, as did the rest of his family, so it seems. I was certainly glad I was not responsible for the eulogy that day: Father Patrick felt, quite rightly, that the situation could not be passed over without a mention. A discrete one, simply suggesting that Eddie was not backward in coming forward concerning the ladies, and that he was a bit of a loveable rogue. That brought a smile to the faces of his wife and family. The ladies all seemed to know about each other and were all very tearful at losing Eddie. The funeral went by without event, and after the interment we went back to a big local pub where everybody, including his lady friends, joined in a drink to Eddie's life. I don't know what Eddie had, but if you could bottle it you would make a fortune. I am certainly not condoning his actions, but you do have to admire his passion!

Passion often rears its head at large funerals and can sometimes be quite loud, although no less respectful than a quiet, sedate funeral. Bermondsey, I am pleased to say, is full of passion, and we rarely have a funeral that does not expose it in some way – often below the surface, but sometimes right in your face and occasionally accompanied by some colourful language, which never offends me.

We arrived at one family's home late one mid-spring afternoon. It was a beautiful day, and we were accompanied by our horses Fred and George, and six following cars. There was the usual display of flowers: the Gates of Heaven, two balls of wool with knitting needles through them because Mum had been a great knitter – the people of Bermondsey often use special arrangements as symbols of somebody's passion and loves in life. There was a 'MUM', a 'NAN', a vacant chair, a broken heart, kisses and lots of posies from the grandchildren, as well as a cross for the lid of the coffin. Many, many wreaths, arrangements and bunches of flowers. As I had the usual amount of time for the funeral, the quantity of flowers did not worry me at all. The boys slowly went about their work with great skill, and when I was completely satisfied with the final display, I began to organise the family and the car list for the travel to the funeral.

At this point, the eldest daughter pulled me aside and asked, 'Barry, I forgot to tell you, but I want to go down the Walworth Road past the top of East Street where Mum used to love to shop, and Marks and Spencer's where she worked for years. Please could we just pass there, would you mind? It would mean a lot to me and the girls.'

Walworth Road was a fair bit off our normal route and would definitely make me late, but I could see how important this was to the family and, well, it was something that just had to be done - simple things like passing familiar places can make or break a funeral. I told her of course not to worry, it would be done. Thrilled by my response, she called out to the girls - all the daughters and granddaughters of the family - 'Don't worry, Barry's got it under control - he's gonna pass East Street and Mum's old workplace.'

With everybody happy and safely in the cars, and a phone call having been made to the cemetery telling them that we would be a few minutes late, we were all set to go. I paged the funeral (walking in front) in the normal fashion along Abbey Street and left into Tower Bridge Road, making our way towards the Elephant and Castle and Walworth Road. Just as we were arriving at East Street, I got down from the horses and again paged the funeral along to the top of East Street, where I stopped for a moment out of respect, removing my hat, as did the horseman and all the drivers. Just opposite East Street was a man with a loud-hailer preaching words of impending doom to the planet but without the respect to stop for a moment in silence and acknowledge the funeral. I felt it my duty to wander across and ask him politely to observe a few moments of silence out of respect for the funeral and the deceased. After a little negotiation, he agreed. Walking back to the front of the funeral, I took the cortège on another 50–100 yards and stopped outside Marks and Spencer's, putting my head round the door just to let them know the funeral was there. Two or three of the staff came out and stood in silence, as did I, as a mark of respect.

What I did not know was that my actions were causing quite a lot of excitement in the first car. The daughter was elated – that I had done exactly what she asked without any fuss at all, that I had managed to silence the harbinger of doom on the far side of the road, and that I had stopped right outside the door of Marks and Spencer's and got some of the staff to come out. Paul, the driver, told me they were saying, 'Ah look, we've come just the way I wanted, look girls!' 'Oh yeah, Mum, brilliant ain't it?'

''Ere girls, he shut that silly old fool up, that's right an' all. Hold your noise,' the daughter cried from the window. 'That's my mum, have a bit of respect. Oh no, he's only gone and stopped right outside the door. No, he's going in. Oh, gawd help us! Oh bloody hell! He's only gone and got all the girls out. Look, 'ere's me mum's mate. Oi! Bal, you're the dogs' – a Bermondsey abbreviation for 'you're the best'.

A few moments later, I walked off. As the funeral cars passed Marks and Spencer's, they waved out to the girls, full of tears, very proud and overwhelmed by the respect the staff showed. As we arrived at the cemetery, the daughter jumped out of the car, ran up to me with a big kiss and said, 'No one can touch you, Bal, you're the absolute dogs. The governor. Soddin' brilliant! Just what I wanted. Thanks, Bal.'

I had really only done my job, but exactly as she had wanted. They were a lovely family, and I will never forget their open passion and the courage they had, quite rightly, to display it in their own way. You know exactly where you stand with people like this, and I respect and love them for it. The daughter's parting words were, 'Bal, you stopped all the flippin' traffic. You done me, Mum and me girls proud.' Is there a better way to say thank you? I have often been described as the precious parts of a dog and I consider it to be a great compliment! I feel the same way towards my own staff, absolute stars, each and every one of them – the dogs.

A quieter kind of passion greeted us one afternoon on a funeral that began at our head office in Culling Road. It was a small funeral, just the hearse and one limousine, very few flowers and only six people in attendance. The next of kin who was arranging and supervising the funeral was the daughter of the deceased, an elderly gentleman who, although he had never lived in the area, had passed away in the local private hospital. We had been recommended to the family, who were quite happy to have the funeral, a cremation, conducted by us in South London. The man's ten-year-old granddaughter, Libby, had been born blind and was attending the funeral with her mother. Her mother was quite wonderful with her and described everything – the colours and designs of the flowers, what the men were wearing, the colours of the cars and what they looked like, all our cars being two-tone black and burgundy with burgundy carpets and black seats. Libby's mother described every detail to her, and we were all taken by this brilliant young lady who had a great zest for life in every way, with the kind of beautiful smile that you never forget. Libby never stopped asking questions or smiling. She may not have been given the gift of sight in this world, but she possessed so many other truly beautiful gifts.

Lee was the limousine driver that day, and anybody who has met Lee in my other books or in the television series will know him as a 'cheeky chappy' who is extremely good at his job. Now Lee has his own passions too, those at work being his car and, most of all, having clean windows. Lee's windows are always immaculate as he spends hours cleaning them. Anybody who touches them drives him mad. I doubt Lee will ever forgive me for this, but I asked Libby's mum if Libby would like to touch the car to feel its shape and texture. Libby overheard this and said, 'Yes please.'

So we led her up to Lee's car, and she walked all around with her hands feeling the pattern of the wings, the bonnet, the radiator, and then moving around to the doors and – yes, you've got it – the windows. I have to admit that I fully encouraged this! In reality, Lee, who has children of his own, was really quite proud to show Libby around his car and explain how everything worked, but he could not help cringing as she went towards his windows to touch them. 'That's right, my darling, there's the windows', he said, moving her swiftly on to another part of the car. Afterwards, I told Libby's mum all about Lee's obsession. She laughed and told Libby, who laughed with her. A little girl's courage and Lee's obsession with his windows are just another small example of how passion drives people.

People's passions often become an addictive part of their life, sometimes more important than life itself, as is often the case with football. After all, it was the late great Bill Shankley who said that football was not a matter of life and death but far more important than that. To Harry Redknapp, the manager of Portsmouth, it really is that serious, and his passion totally governs his moods. He commented after Portsmouth lost a pre-Christmas match (sorry about the language here): 'Christmas can come and go. I don't give a shit now. We will train Christmas Eve, Christmas Day, every day. I don't give a shit about Christmas. I'm the most miserable man alive when we lose. My wife's Christmas is over today and she knows it!' Something tells me he was wearing his Christmas dinner that year.

In my younger life, and still sometimes today, I make kind of superstitious trade-offs. In the television series, ultimately in front of millions of people - I hope that many were watching! - you might have seen me miss a penalty playing football. I told myself afterwards not to worry. Maybe my miss might lead to Liverpool winning the Premiership next year and Millwall getting promoted to it (or winning the Cup - stranger things have happened, and almost did while I was writing this book!). In hindsight, ridiculous of course, but a brief consolation. You will have gathered by now, especially if you have read any of my other books, that football is a great passion of mine too.

I once had the fine honour of meeting Sir Bobby Robson, certainly one of the greatest managers this country has ever known. Now in his seventies, he is still driven by a great passion for the game and is still very successfully managing Newcastle United. I attended one of Bobby's many coaching courses back in the 1970s when he was manager of Ipswich Town. Sir Bobby had a great friendship with the chairman of Ipswich Town, his boss of course, who owned the club. This man, family excepted, had three great passions – Ipswich Town, the huge brewery that had made him wealthy and, last but definitely not least, his donkey sanctuary.

Now Sir Bobby was at the time one of the first managers to buy foreign players, having in his squad two Dutch players, Frans Thijssen and Arnold Muhren. This was the time of the World Cup, and Bobby had travelled with his chairman's blessing to look for players to add to his squad. It was also the days of the great Dutch team that was to star Johan Cruyff and a time when telegrams were often used. Sir Bobby watched Cruyff play in the opening game and immediately knew he was a player with special qualities. Excitedly, Sir Bobby sent a telegram back to the chairman: 'Get a bank overdraft and mortgage the club I have seen a real star stop.' The return telegram said, 'No problem club mortgaged just buy him and bring him to Ipswich stop.'

Spurred on by this reply, Robson again watched Cruyff play – a sensation. Sir Bobby immediately realised that Cruyff would cost a fortune so he sent a second telegram: 'Cruyff a sensation better sell the brewery stop.' To his surprise, he had an immediate reply, which read 'Brewery on market just get Cruyff stop.'

After the third game, it was clear that Cruyff was the outstanding player of the tournament, probably the best player in the world at the time, so Sir Bobby sent another telegram: 'Cruyff the best player I have ever seen you better sell donkeys as well stop.' Almost immediately, he received the simple reply, 'Sod Cruyff I'm keeping the donkeys stop': an example of one passion outweighing another. And a fun example of what can be a serious subject.

Passion can also be aroused in the shape of fears, often those with their roots in superstition. For example, when I conduct a funeral, let's say through the Blue, a shopping street in my beloved Bermondsey, tipping my hat to people as I go, some of the older people remember the old superstition – if an undertaker tips his hat to you, you're gonna be next. They often share a joke with me over this, but I know one or two do feel a little afraid somewhere inside and need to laugh it off. Others say that when petals fall from the back of the hearse as it is pulling away from the cemetery, someone is sure to follow. So I always make very sure that there are no petals falling off the end of the hearse as we leave any cemetery or crematorium. School children and even some older people hold their collars as a funeral passes in the old superstition that they might be next. This is from an old nursery rhyme, 'Hold your collar, waller, waller, waller never catch a fever', although I am sure that none of these youngsters know this. So does superstition drive us passionately in some way? Or is it just the fear of what could or will be in the end?

A colleague of mine had a very unusual case in America (where else?!) of a gentleman, Geoff, who had lost Sylvia, his bride-to-be and partner for some twenty years, only days before they were to be married. Geoff insisted on going ahead with the wedding in the funeral home. There was Sylvia, lying in the casket in her wedding dress. Geoff stood alongside her in his wedding suit. As he slipped the ring on to her finger, he commented, 'This was to be the happiest day of our lives.' He leaned over to kiss her and could only say that everything seemed so unreal. The wedding of course could not be truly recognised in law, but the union was blessed by a priest. Geoff ended the ceremony by sitting next to his new wife, as he wanted her to be known, and finally said, 'I wonder if she knew that we had got married. I do hope so.' Whether you think that this is right or wrong, you have to admire that kind of passion and devotion. If there is a God, and I am sure there is, Geoff and Sylvia are as married as married can be, surreal and strange as it feels, even if it is in a way a little charming. There are always questions when something different takes place; some will say it is very weird, others that it is a beautiful thing. And there are those who say it could only happen in America.

Now, there is no one more passionate than me when it comes to work, or so I thought until I heard from a colleague of mine about Fred, who had worked in the same publishing firm for over thirty years. He was always the first guy in the office each morning and, without fail, the last to leave at night. He kept himself to himself in the office and rarely spoke to anybody. He was the sort of person who totally absorbed himself in his work and had little time in his life for anything else. Fred lived alone and had little or no family, so it was not unusual for the staff to see him sitting in his office in the same position day in, day out.

On this occasion though, Fred's passion seemed out of control – out of his control, anyway. His boss, Mike, went in one Saturday morning to collect some papers, and out of the corner of his eye happened to catch Fred sitting at his desk. He went along to Fred, tapped him on the shoulder and said, 'What are you doing in today, Fred?' But there was no reply. An autopsy report from the coroner revealed that Fred had been dead in the same position for about five days, yet nobody had noticed. I think this story is really sad and reminds us to keep an eye out for our co-workers and occasionally give them a little nudge. I suppose the moral of the story could be not to work too hard because nobody notices anyway, but the real message is probably that this is the way Fred, God rest his soul, would have liked to have gone, sitting in his favourite chair at his favourite desk doing the job he loved. I'm just glad the office was air-conditioned or the other staff would definitely have had to sit up and take notice.

The most passionate of funerals, however, seem to crop up when you least expect them. Sam was a great guy whose amazing whole life had brimmed with passion. He had had a fantastically varied career, often working on exhibitions like the Ideal Homes Exhibition. He sometimes acted as a courier on his beloved bike, but perhaps his greatest passion was being a part-time actor, having appeared, albeit briefly, in many James Bond films and television series such as *The Bill* and *Minder*. Sam was just one of those extras who cropped up everywhere and thoroughly enjoyed every moment of it. Jenny, his partner, said that he had been in more James Bond films than James Bond himself (well, I knew what she meant!). Sam had been diagnosed with cancer and, as you would expect of such a man, had bravely fought every moment of it with the kind of passion some people can only dream of. Having lived his life to the full in the true belief that happiness is found not at the end of the journey but along the way, Sam finally and gracefully accepted his fate, with a parting wish of a funeral to remember.

It may sound strange to say but Sam's funeral was one of the happiest I have ever attended, a fantastic tribute to his life from the people who loved him. Even though he was terminally ill, he and Jenny would never miss one single episode of our television programme *Don't Drop the Coffin*. He thought it was 'fantastic' – his and Jenny's words, not mine – and he insisted to Jenny that I was to conduct his funeral when he died (a great privilege and a great honour to be asked). She said she couldn't agree more, and at his passing came straight in to make the funeral arrangements. She had seen Father Alan, priest from the Most Holy Trinity Church at Dockhead, who always sings at our annual memorial service, performing 'Can You Feel the Love Tonight?', the theme from the film *Lion King*, and was desperate for him to sing this at Sam's funeral. A little nervously, Father Alan agreed. It probably didn't help that, after the television series, we had nicknamed him 'Simba' after the lion in the film.

As we arrived at the family home to pick up the funeral, Jenny ran towards me and greeted me with a big kiss and a cuddle. She was determined that today would be a joyous day, a day nobody would forget. A friend of Sam's, on a motorbike, was ready to follow the cortège, and everywhere there were faces that you have seen on the television but could not quite put a name to. It was a fantastic atmosphere. We quietly arranged the many floral tributes, called everybody ceremonially to the cars one by one, handed out the funeral travel flags for the bonnet of each car, collected Father Alan and left together for the crematorium.

We had a double slot at the crematorium so we had plenty of time to manoeuvre around the service. As we pulled into the gates of Honor Oak Crematorium, we were totally overwhelmed by the number of people waiting for the funeral. At this point, I think that Father Alan's knees were knocking together and he was wondering what he had done – although very accomplished, he admits to being very nervous in these situations when singing, and he was also conducting the funeral service so he had a lot to be responsible for. I told him, 'Don't worry, you're going to be great. I'm coming in, and I'll stand right behind you, and I'll make sure that the music goes on at the correct time and everything flows as it should. Don't worry.' Luckily, we always work together very well, but I had to think of something to calm him down.

The funeral began with us carrying Sam's coffin into the chapel to the unaccompanied singing of 'You'll Never Walk Alone'. After five minutes of settling down the enormous number of people who were attending, we closed the door of the chapel and the service officially began. One of Sam's closest friends spoke very eloquently and with much humour about Sam's life, to everyone's great enjoyment. It was one of those rare occasions when everybody attending the funeral was of one mind. There was a special feeling that everybody was joining in with the moment. Nobody disapproved, and everybody knew that this was Sam's way of doing things. It was fantastic.

Next to speak was Sam's best friend, a stand-up comic from the West End clubs. He was terribly nervous and was not sure whether he could do it. He stood in front of people every night and ran his routine without a problem, but standing in front of his best friend, and many other friends, at such a time was almost too much for the guy. He said to me, 'Look, if I can't do this when the time comes, please just say something for me.' I assured him that he would be fine, that he would have the courage, and I was not wrong. He started a hilarious routine about his best friend with something like, 'If it hadn't been for pickpockets in the West End, Sam wouldn't have had a sex life.' Everybody, including Jenny, just roared with laughter. Sam's friend went from strength to strength, and ended nearly in tears himself – tears partly of laughter, partly of loss, but certainly of passion.

'Simba' was next up, singing to the pre-recorded music of 'Can You Feel the Love Tonight?' He sang it as well as I have ever known him sing it, with great charisma, singing directly to Jenny and often moving over to Sam's coffin to involve Sam in the service. As he finished, everybody stood and clapped with overwhelming emotion and passion. We finally finished with everybody dancing round the coffin, their arms round each other and singing at the top of their voices, while we played Sam's favourite party song, 'New York, New York', a final goodbye to Sam. It was one of the most moving, emotional funerals I have ever attended, a totally unexpected experience.

As you can see from this, funerals no longer have to stick completely to tradition. They are now usually tailored towards people's lives, which then involves the passion of the death itself. As Jenny lives locally, I have seen her several times since Sam's funeral, and every time I do I cannot help but tell her how moved I was by that day. You never know it all, you never see it all and you can never have done it all, but Sam's funeral was one I was never ever going to forget.

Well, what of me? I am now fifty-three years of age and I believe that I have lost none of the passion that has carried me through life. It has sometimes been my only salvation and my only redeeming feature. It pushed me through my early days at school when I truly found it hard to learn. On the occasions on which I did succeed and found myself on top in life, it pushed me that bit further, exciting me, taking me, as they say in America, 'the extra nine yards' with the will to get there. When I have felt utterly alone and in my bleakest times, passion has been a friend, because in the middle of tragedy we are alone, no matter what is going on around us. At such times, there are always people around to help us, but in the end only *you* have the power within you and you have to stand alone and go on with life whatever it may bring.

Passion opens us to tears of pain when we lose somebody. Tears of happiness at a birth or a joyous occasion. Tears of despair at the darker times in our lives. It has the power to push you on through and immerses you when you find love in your life. Our family and friends, however few or distant they may be, are probably the one thing we all share passionately in common. After my family, my own two great passions are Albin's and football. Both still excite me after all these years, even though now the mind may be willing but the body is struggling to keep up.

So now we have looked at passion in many guises: loving, sad, addictive, superstitious, angry, loud, in life and in death. However passion raises its head, you have got to admire it, because without it we have only a shell of emptiness. Passion certainly makes things happen in this world. If you have passion, you have 75 per cent of what you need to succeed – the other 25 per cent can be learnt. As for the next world, we will just have to wait and see, but I won't tip my hat to you just yet!

2
IT'S NOTHING TO WORRY ABOUT

Life would not be life as we know it if nothing ever went wrong. Funerals, which for me have always been as much about life as about death, are of course not immune from human, mechanical or third-party error. In fact, they can sometimes be fated. I know from experience that when things go wrong at funerals, it is usually the end result of a small chain of reactions, as I call them. Let me try to explain. Let's say, for example, that you have a busy day in front of you; with that thought at the back of your mind, you arrive at work already slightly stressed and under pressure. Now, if you allow that stress and pressure to change your regular procedure in any way, even in terms of the smallest detail, I believe that you have started a chain reaction that could lead to a major error. Think about an error that has happened in your daily life when you originally had control of it and trace it back – I bet I'm right.

So how can we avoid that kind of chain reaction? The truth is that we sometimes can't, but if we stick to the normal

21

procedures and are thorough in all we do, we narrow the margin of possibility of error. Of course, people (including me) never expect funerals to go wrong, and in reality they rarely do, but when they do the effect on the bereaved is multiplied a hundred-fold, usually well out of proportion to the problem itself. As I understand that, I always strive for perfection.

We know, however, that perfection is not always possible. Things do occasionally go wrong. The real issue is how we handle them when they do. When something goes wrong, the most important first rule is: **Don't look to blame anyone**. The second rule is: **Put it right at all costs**, and the third rule is: **Try to put the welfare of the family you are serving first** (there will be plenty of time for 'post-mortems' later). Today, we are more usually referred to as funeral directors rather than undertakers, 'funeral directors' sounding a more professional and perhaps gentler introduction to the work we do or the vocation we have. People will always understand that mistakes happen and things go wrong, but they will be looking to us as the conductors of that funeral – the virtuosos, as the Japanese call us – to solve the problem with the least amount of fuss and the most consideration possible, yet with a gentleness that these days can rarely be found in service industries.

So how do we project that gentleness, perhaps more accurately described as a cushion softening the reality of the situation? How do we solve the problems? For instance, if our Rolls-Royce limousine will not start, we are unlikely to say that it is broken; we would probably be more comfortable with 'it simply failed to continue'. If we are late at the cemetery or crematorium, we would probably say that 'we are never late, just slightly delayed' or 'just not rushing'. Speaking as the only funeral director in the country who has never been late arriving at a cemetery or crematorium (ouch, I lie!), I would have to say I am an expert, but, as the saying goes, an expert is only yesterday's has-been. Well, call me what you like, but when it comes to funerals I am at least completely sincere, I promise you.

Nobody wants to admit that they have made a mistake; that is, after all, human nature. But we have to realise our mistakes quickly, deal with them and accept them, particularly when you are talking about a funeral, for which there is never a dress rehearsal. Let's take a look at the things that do go and have gone wrong around life, death and funerals themselves. They are varied, sometimes amusing and often almost too strange to be true. There are, for example, technical hitches.

People who know me will know that I have no great love for the sound of the bagpipes, although I like people who play them very much; they are usually great characters. One time, we had one piper booked for two funerals in one day. The morning funeral was a beautiful Irish funeral, and there was the piper dressed in all his Irish finery walking smartly at double time just in front of the funeral, playing very well, I thought – if the bagpipes could ever be played very well, that is. By the afternoon he was ready for a second funeral, this time for a Scots person. The piper had had to made a quick change, and there he was in all his Scots finery walking at slow pace to 'Flowers of the Forest' in front of the funeral. When the funeral had gone into the chapel, I asked him how he could cover both nationalities. 'Easy, mate,' he said. 'I'm neither Irish nor Scottish, I'm a Cockney. I just make a living out of impersonating them.' Well, I had to laugh. What a character. Especially as he then added that he did not like the bagpipes either. Typical Cockney cheek, that one.

When something goes technically wrong with the bagpipes, they sound like a strangled cat being swung round the top of your head, or how I would imagine that to sound anyway. This caterwauling comes from the piper chasing the bottom of the bagpipes when the bottom of the bag and the chanter fly apart, causing, in the quiet serenity of the funeral service, a screech like a crying banshee, completely out of place. The only thing to do if this happens is to grab the piper and remove him and the bagpipes as quickly as possible!

Some technical problems can be anticipated, for example by back-up equipment. You should always have a spare CD and tape player in case the main one fails. And batteries in case the power goes off. Also, have a few spare tapes and CDs of different music. Holy water is also a must in case the priest forgets his, or sometimes to save him the worry of having to remember it in the first place. Have a spare service book in case the priest turns up without one (not usual, but it has happened). Always have a camera available too, in case people want some photographs to be taken.

All this is good preparation for avoiding technical hitches, but an Australian colleague told me of one that I don't think he could have avoided. At the hottest time of the year he had a huge funeral, and the crematorium was greatly overcrowded because of the sheer number of people who wanted to get inside to hear the service. Unfortunately, it was also so hot that the air-conditioning broke down. It was impossible for my colleague to open the windows as they were completely sealed to get the best benefit from the air-conditioning. One man became so overwhelmed by the heat that he collapsed and broke his jawbone. This man then sued the funeral director for some $14,000 for breach of duty and breach of contract with negligence. What could my poor colleague do?

This was hardly his fault, but as he is the contractor, people regard everything that goes wrong as his fault. That's the plight of the funeral director. (Thank goodness we are not a nation of suers here, not yet anyway.)

If the minister uses the wrong name at a funeral, you would say it is unforgivable, and I would agree. In the end, however, it becomes our fault even though we have given him the correct name in writing: as he is subcontracted by us, it is our responsibility. That's what we do, and that's why you employ us. But be reasonable, please, as we are only human!

I felt genuinely sorry for my Australian colleague, but that was nothing compared with what happened to the manager of a huge basketball team in America (I digress here, but bear with me). After the manager lost the game to local rivals, the owner of the basketball club is reported to have burst into his office and screamed at him, 'If we ever lose like that again to a team like that, I'm gonna kill your dog and eat it.'

The manager replied, puzzled, 'I don't have a dog.'

The next week, the manager received a basket with a small dog inside it; around the dog's neck was a note saying, 'Don't get too attached.' Now that is serious stuff. Thank goodness we have never gone that far in the funeral profession.

Just as sad, though, was an experience I had with a funeral not long ago. It is not unusual to have a prisoner released from prison to attend a family funeral. Prisoners are then always very well guarded, usually by being handcuffed to a prison officer with at least two other officers and a driver in attendance. It is always very difficult for the prisoner himself, his or her family and indeed the officers who have to attend. If prisoners are well behaved, the officers will usually bring them to the house, let them attend the funeral as it leaves the house, take them to the church, on to the cemetery or crematorium and, very occasionally, briefly back to the house, but this always depends on the category of the prisoner and certainly how he or she behaves. Whatever happens, this is a very emotional time for everybody, and I always feel sorry for the family when they have to say goodbye. It is almost like a double bereavement.

In this particular incident, the prisoner was taken directly to the church and was waiting just across the road from it with two prison officers, handcuffed to one of them. As we arrived, the family got out of the cars and were crossing the road to go towards their son. One fellow, not known to the family or me, had already approached the prisoner and was having a word with him. I turned to see this fellow put his arms around the prisoner as if to say goodbye affectionately. Then I heard screaming, shouting and a scuffle; all hell had broken loose. It seems that this chap had tried to pass a package to the prisoner, who – let's make this clear – did not want it anyway. The prison officer and his colleague saw what was going on and immediately seized the package. The father, who also saw what was going on, immediately punched the other guy squarely on the chin. And who could blame him? 'Well done, mate,' I thought. The guy did not retaliate but simply ran off.

This had, however, spoilt the whole day for the family, for the prisoner himself, who had not caused this to happen, and of course for the prison officers, whose job was made twice as hard because of the incident. The prison officers were then obliged to take the prisoner directly back to prison after the church service and not allow him to participate any further in the funeral. This was heartbreaking for his family, for himself and for everybody concerned. It also made my job almost impossible, because you can imagine how difficult it was to calm the family down and get everybody into the right frame of mind to continue with the funeral Mass. People who call themselves friends are sometimes not friends at all. I know that young man's father quite well, and I admire him enormously for his actions.

But where there is tragedy, comedy is never very far away. We were recently asked to conduct a funeral near Darenth in Kent, an area I do not know very well but which is more familiar to my sons, Simon and Jonathan, who had already sorted out the route. Simon was driving the hearse, with me as conductor beside him; Jonathan was driving the first limousine. Off we went down the A2 towards Darenth, coming off at the exit for the Bluewater shopping centre, which would take us into Darenth and the address we were heading for. Luckily, we had none of the family with us at this point.

Simon knew what he was doing, but he accidentally took the first exit from the roundabout instead of the second. This took us down towards the shopping centre. At this point, Simon knew how to get out of this, but I didn't. Undeterred, I took control, as always. 'Simon, come off at the next exit here.'

'No,' he said, 'we'll go under there, Dad, and we can come up and around.'

'Do you know that, though?' I asked.

'Yes, I'm pretty sure, Dad,' he said.

'No, turn off here, Simon.' I could see a roundabout below and thought we could go round the roundabout, back up and past where we had just come from to take the correct exit. With that, I put him in two minds, which is never a good thing to do to somebody. 'Quick, quick, to the left,' I said. So to the left we went, and – yes, you've guessed it – we were now going into the Bluewater shopping centre, somewhere I had always said I would never shop anyway!

It is a great privilege to be Simon's dad and boss, but being both of those things I immediately blamed him (breaking my first rule, even if only in jest). Quite rightly, he was not concerned with the blame – he just wanted to avoid Bluewater. Fortunately, Simon goes shopping there quite often and knew we could avoid going into the shopping centre or its car park by going round the roundabout as I had originally thought and back up. This he did, bless him, but he has never yet lived the incident down. You see, I kept quiet when they ribbed him, so I am now openly confessing in print that it was really my fault and I was just using boss's privilege at the time. We were only a couple of minutes late and nobody was distressed. Quite the contrary, in fact, as when we looked in the mirror at my younger son Jonathan in the car behind, we could see from his expression that he knew exactly what we had done and was enjoying every moment of his father and his brother having made such a silly mistake.

At least misdirection can be overcome and fended off. One problem that I defy anyone to be immune from is that of the bodily dysfunction of the 'runs', diarrhoea. Everybody reading this book will have experienced it and will sympathise, because when you have got to go, you have just got to go. You are, without doubt, in a very vulnerable position, particularly when you are conducting a funeral with a rather bad bout of the condition. On this particular day I was suffering from a serious case of it, and the circumstances prevailing at the time meant that there was no one else who could conduct this particular funeral. There was no way out for me. It was a Mass at Dockhead, to be conducted for a family whom I have known most of my life. My friend Father Alan, the presiding priest, knew my position and did not know whether to laugh or cry. We arrived – only just from my point of view – at the church for the Mass. I asked my son to look after the family while I, as usual, went to see the priest and use the amenities quickly. As I went through the Sanctuary, Father Alan took one look at me and said, 'Barry, you don't look well.'

'Can't stop, Alan,' I said, 'nature calls!' and went as fast as I could through into Alan's house and straight to the toilet.

I appeared a few minutes later and explained my predicament. Alan was sympathetic as always and agreed to leave the house door open so I could use the toilet. He even offered me a spare pair of laces in case I wanted to tie my trousers up (always the sympathetic friend). I declined the offer but appreciated the gesture! I was able to spend much of the Mass in the toilet while my son kept a careful eye on proceedings, but towards the end, where I prepare and assist with the thurible, I had no option but to keep my cheeks tightly squeezed and stand motionless. Surely, there was nothing left in me by now?

Like a true professional, I stuck to my task. I placed the coffin gently on to the hearse, seated the family in the cars, walked slowly back into the church and walked smartly down the centre aisle, reaching the toilet just in time – only just in time, believe me. By now, I felt that the worst was over. I had taken two pills, and as I would be able to sit for most of the journey, which is usually more comfortable when you are in such a condition, I felt that all would be well, as indeed it was.

As we arrived at the graveside and placed the coffin at the side of the grave, pulling the webs through the handles with which we would lower the coffin, I took up my traditional position, legs apart across the head of the grave to hold both head webs and steady them during their journey down into the grave. At this time, Father Alan was directly behind me and I did note that he moved swiftly to the left, perhaps to avoid being in the line of fire should all go wrong. As I crouched down and lowered the coffin directly into the grave, I feared the worst – one false move and all would be lost. Fortunately the moment passed without incident. While we were walking back to the church, Father Alan remarked to me that he too had feared the worst and prayed 'Jesus, Joseph and Mary, don't let the heavens open, and if it's your will protect us all from this fate.' Luckily, his prayer was answered, and although at the time it was a painful experience we often laugh about it now. The family, quite rightly, had no idea what was happening. I felt like a true professional to the end – but which end, you might well ask.

Sometimes such near-uncontrollability is threatened just by the sheer size of a funeral. One West Indian funeral that we conducted was, like most West Indian funerals, a fabulous event, but this particular funeral had the added responsibility of being one of the largest attended funerals that I have ever seen outside a state one. There were literally hundreds of cars. We had horses, twelve limousines, a huge church service and a massive procession to the graveside, so we were naturally a little behind schedule, even though I had allowed what I considered to be ample time. As I arrived at the cemetery, just after four o'clock and a little over an hour late, I looked helplessly at the superintendent, who just smiled and said, 'Don't worry, Barry, I got your message. I completely understand. There are already hundreds of the family here by the grave; you must have had a terrible afternoon.' Terrible wasn't the right word because it was a fabulous funeral to be attending, but I knew what he meant. It was definitely stressful.

The final interment at the graveside went beautifully and without a hitch. Doves were released with as much passion as I have ever seen, and we began the traditional hymn-singing and back-filling of the grave, which can take up to an hour. Usually, the flowers are then finally placed on the grave, and over the next fifteen to twenty minutes people leave quietly and go back to the reception at a hall somewhere. On this occasion, however, they had decided that the party would be right there at the graveside. The traditional bottles of rum were broken open, and there was a strong smell of ganja in the air, giving a new meaning to the idea of passive smoking. Everyone broke into merry song, and the party was on.

At about six o'clock, the superintendent came over and said, 'I'm going to have to lock the gates if they don't leave now.' I suggested he told them himself, but he smiled, thanked me and declined. So I walked slowly over and suggested it would be a good time to leave as people would be waiting at the final venue. The family, however, simply invited me to join them for a drink, which out of politeness I accepted – the smallest tipple from a tin of Coca-Cola – while telling them that the gates were to be closed in the next ten minutes and we really did have to go. Their reply came back in West Indian rhythm and verse: 'Hey man, relax, be cool. Him can lock da gate, we stay ere all nite and have da party ere, no problem man.'

What can you say to that? 'I'll make a deal with you,' I replied. 'I'll keep the gates open for another half an hour, and then we'll all go together and have a drink back at the hall.'

'Hey man, that's fine, you cool, you da man, we do that.'

I begged the superintendent to give us a few extra minutes to clear the cemetery, and he agreed, seeing my dilemma. True to their word, the family and friends left the cemetery

thirty or forty minutes later. We had a final farewell at the
hall and made our way back to the garage at about half past
seven in the evening. In the end, a situation that could have
got out of hand actually ended very nicely, thanks to
everyone's patience and goodwill. One to remember that
was, man!

I have always believed that, as a conductor of funerals, you
must always be prepared. Expect the unexpected. I am fully
prepared to stop the traffic for a funeral. I will step in to be a
DJ (although the younger members of staff are usually the
masters of that task). Or undertake a reading or a eulogy. Be
Master of Ceremonies. Whatever it takes, really, but what
happened to me on a funeral a few months ago was certainly
a first.

It was a local funeral of quite a reasonable size that went
back to our local Fisher Club, where we have a friendly bar
and lounge and visitors can be well looked after. We arrived
back at about half past twelve: just time for a friendly drink, a
nice buffet, tea, coffee, what I would call a gentle wake.
Sometimes the food is arranged by our own catering department, sometimes the Fisher Club lays on a few sandwiches,
sometimes the family take care of their own catering arrangements. On this occasion, there was, for the first time, a
complete misunderstanding. We had booked the Fisher Club,
they were all ready, and the bar staff were all set to go. The
family had looked at and discussed our menus but had never
come back to confirm, and no one had spoken to the staff of
the Fisher Club. One half of the family thought the other half
had done that. It was merely a misunderstanding between
them and us, and going back to my first golden rule, there
was no blame to be apportioned, just a problem needing to
be solved.

So there we were, about sixty people in all. Plenty of drink but not a morsel of food. Suddenly I'm the catering manager, and that's when a local knowledge of eating habits can be a great help. 'Right lads,' I said, 'we've got to get some food together quickly.' I sent one of the boys down to the local fish shop and arranged twenty portions of chips and thirty saveloys. Then I phoned the office and asked Jackie to get one of the girls to fly over to Tesco, only a few minutes away at Surrey Quays, to buy some ready-made sandwiches. Jimmy, the barman at the Fisher Club, was busy behind the bar getting the urn going to lay on tea and coffee as quickly as possible. Then it was down to the local baker to get a dozen French sticks and three large flans and cheesecakes. Jackie thought on her feet and arranged some pre-packed salads as well as the final magic ingredient – jellied eels from the local fish stall (a must at local funerals).

In twenty minutes, we had a feast fit for a king – a Bermondsey Pearly King, that is. By the time it had all arrived, I had the tables covered in white paper tablecloths, and within minutes it was all laid out. Only the immediate family knew that there had been a problem at all. Every morsel went, but I must have lost about two pounds in that half an hour: whether or not it had been my fault, I would still feel responsible. As for the family, they were absolutely delighted and were having quite a laugh at my running around like Keith Floyd in the kitchen.

Kindness goes a long way to sorting difficult situations, but sometimes even the kindest of gestures can cause great problems. We had just collected the repatriated remains of a soldier who had died in action abroad, something that I have always considered a very great honour to be involved with. The arrival of any soldier is greeted with great ceremonial honours and enormous respect by all concerned. We have to provide a hearse for the collection of the deceased to continue his or her repatriation in accordance with the family's request, returning the soldier to the family's nominated funeral director.

In this particular instance, the soldier was being returned to northern England, and Reg, one of our most trusted and longest-serving chauffeurs, was responsible for his safe return. Driving very carefully, as he always does, he was overtaken by a people-carrier containing a Chinese family. Now there is a tradition that I have experienced many times when conducting Chinese funerals that the family pass over what is called lucky money. In a gesture of kindness and tradition, this is exactly what this family on the motorway did. Every one of them leaned out of a window and threw the lucky money on to the road in front of the hearse. Many of the coins bounced up again, hitting the bonnet and chipping the paint. One 50p piece even hit the windscreen directly in front of Reg, gouging out a huge divot and forcing him to pull over. Not realising that they had caused any problems, the party continued on their journey, leaving us to respray the bonnet of the hearse and repair the windscreen. For Reg, the lucky money could have been very unlucky; but who knows, forcing Reg to stop might have changed the course of events and saved him from a serious accident further up the road. Later that day and without any further delay, the soldier was returned to his family.

All sorts of consequences can arise from such incidents and delays. A local minister, who has since retired, once caused just such a change in events. The minister, a colourful local character with a bladder problem, had not declared to me when I arrived at the funeral that he was there or that he was travelling with us. I fully expected him to be at the cemetery. We arranged all the family flowers on the hearse and cars. Arranged all the family seating – nearest, dearest and eldest first. The eldest son then locked the front door with a mortice lock, telling me that everybody had left the flat. I paged the funeral away from the flat and around into Southwark Park Road, on to which the flats backed.

As I was walking along in front of the funeral – cane, top hat, gloves – I heard a cry from high above me. There was the minister, hanging over the balcony, shouting, 'Barry, Barry, I'm locked in. Wait. Please get me out, don't leave me.' It seems that the poor gentleman had at the last moment taken to the toilet. As he had previously been seated in the corner of the living room, the family just thought he had left. I did not know he was there, and the mortice lock on the front door prevented his leaving. The family, who were really lovely, were tickled pink by what had happened. I retrieved the keys, let the minister out and re-locked the door before we proceeded with the funeral. The minister, of course, could not stop apologising, but the family simply said, 'Aah, you've made Mum's day. We'll never forget this.' No problem, but what a sight he was hanging over the balcony.

Unfortunately though, those few minutes of delay really changed the day's course of events – causing the chain reaction I mentioned above. We arrived at the cemetery some fifteen minutes later than we should have done as we had got caught in the start of the rush-hour traffic. The knock-on effect meant that we were then fifteen minutes late leaving the chapel and arriving at the graveside.

Now Tom, a very fit and helpful grave-digger, had been draining some water from the grave. This often needs to be done because the ground there is clay and very wet, particularly in winter. Our being late meant that some water had run into the grave again. Tom, ever helpful, wanted to clear the water, so as we arrived at the grave he was still pumping out. In his haste to shut the noisy machine down, he knocked the top hose off the pump. Freezing cold, filthy water was shot ten feet into the air, spraying everywhere. Tom sacrificed himself by throwing his body across the water jet, which almost lifted him off the ground, the pressure was so great. We all saw the predicament Tom was in, fighting for his position, so we rushed across to try to help in our beautiful black clothes, with putrefied water showering everywhere. Eventually we managed to knock the machine switch off, but by now the whole area – and us too – was saturated; it was all very unpleasant.

Now, fifteen minutes earlier and this chain reaction would not have happened. The minister's wonky bladder in the end created far more water than he had bargained for, more in fact than any of us had bargained for: he had spent a penny and caused a flood. As for Tom, he was bruised, saturated and very smelly but, as he said, 'I couldn't let you down, mate.' Pulling together, we completed the interment, to the family's words of 'What a day!' Since then, I have conducted other funerals for that family, but whenever I see them they always recall the events of that day with humour.

On another occasion, we were at a local cemetery heading for a grave that had been pre-chosen by the family, who had made a visit earlier in the week and picked a particular place. I walked across to the grave that had been dug, only to hear the son shouting behind me, 'It's the wrong grave. It's not the right grave, Barry. The grave I chose is another twenty yards just over here. Look, by my old nan's.'

At a moment like this, your heart stops. Your immediate concern must be for the family and trying in some way to put it right. In this particular instance, it was the misreading of a digit that had caused the problem, so it was all hands on deck. The cemetery immediately accepted the error and organised the opening of the previously chosen grave. I assembled the family and said, 'Look, this is a human error in the office. Somebody has misread a digit on the paper and given the foreman the wrong number. If we are all patient, in the next thirty to forty minutes we will have the grave properly dug and we can carry on with the funeral. You won't be charged for the grave at all, and the cemetery will allow you to reserve a second grave without charge. We are all so sorry that this has happened to you as a family.'

The son retorted, "Ere, that's my dad – buy one, get one free. Ain't it, girls, what do ya think? Buy one, get one free, that's Dad, ain't it?' The son had magically broken the tension, proving again that laughter and tears are all part and parcel of the same emotion. The family suggested carving 'Our dad bought one and got one free' on the gravestone. I'll keep an eye out to see whether they do over the years. In the face of adversity, a little bit of their dad's character had come through at that funeral.

Whatever you encounter, you are only as good as the last funeral you did. I never take it for granted. We are all vulnerable, we can all make mistakes – and yes, we have had cars that wouldn't start. We have had people lost on the way to a funeral. Like every funeral director, we have been late. We have been made late by other funeral directors, and we have made other funeral directors late (we all have to work together). We have had graves that have been wrongly opened. We have had ministers failing to turn up. We have had motor accidents during and on the way back from funerals. We have had people experience heart attacks at a funeral, even somebody who has died at one. We have had fights. I have never yet had a baby born at a funeral, but what an experience that would be.

But, like every other funeral director, what I dread is burying or cremating the wrong deceased. I am absolutely terrified about this, and I have so many fail-safe systems in place, all the way down to my personal check as I get into the hearse, to prevent my nightmare ever becoming reality. That reality would take all the goodness from what we do, as well as destroy me inside. This should not, cannot, must not ever happen, and with God on your side, who could be against you? Everything else we can deal with.

3

MY FIFTEEN MINUTES OF FAME

I guess my real fifteen minutes of fame, as Andy Warhol once called it, began with the publishing of my first book, *Don't Drop the Coffin*. My fifteen minutes seems, however, to have grown and grown. It has truly been quite revealing, yet nothing could have prepared me for the spark of fame, recognition and success that was to be ignited by the television series, also entitled *Don't Drop the Coffin*. This was a six-part, real-life documentary commissioned by Ginger Television and produced by Stephen Joel, someone who has now become a good friend and who has justified my trust in him from the beginning.

Agreeing to do the programme was the result of hours of soul-searching; after all, I was really putting my neck on the block. I had for many years believed that such a programme could really change the nation's perception of death and that people who watched the programme might, if nothing else, be just a little less afraid of death. If I managed to achieve that, and if the public truly saw us as decent, caring people doing a difficult job well and trying – and managing – to make a difference, rather than as the old-fashioned, grim, come-into-my-parlour-said-the-spider-to-the-fly type of funeral director we have been portrayed as over the years, the whole industry might be seen thereafter as the fourth emergency service. And not just F. A. Albin & Sons, but every funeral director in the industry. Funeral directors large and small work very hard for the people they serve at an extremely difficult and vulnerable time, and to be a good funeral director is a true vocation.

I believe that the programme portrayed all I had hoped for, but the recognition that came with it was staggering. A national daily newspaper reported, 'Don't Drop the Coffin ITV1 8.30 p.m. – if Barry Dyer ran the country instead of a funeral business not only would everything run on time but the spin doctors would be out on their ears. Check out his common-sense foreign policy as he flies to Detroit to find out about Cryonics. So watch out Tony Blair.' (I wonder if Tony read it too?)

So huge in fact was the response that I was overwhelmed. We received hundreds of letters of support, e-mails and phone calls. The television company gave us a PR person, Jill Francis, to take care of us, and she was absolutely marvellous. We were offered at least thirty interviews with newspapers, magazines, etc. We were invited on to the morning programme on Channel 5 television, the Terry and Gaby programme. All these requests had to be vetted by Jill, and we selected a few magazines, newspapers and media interviews that she was happy with. They booked me a day at the BBC where I was linked into live and recorded radio programmes, about sixteen of them if I remember rightly, throughout the day. I was invited on to The Salon for a haircut, massage and manicure, literally anything I wanted. I went on the Mick Brown Capital Gold morning radio show, which I enjoyed immensely. Mick is a Millwall fan too, and I had actually undertaken a family funeral for him. I think he enjoyed the half-hour as much as I did.

I took part in television's *The Hundred Worst Records of All Time*, talking about some of the tunes that had been used at funerals. I did lots of phone-in programmes, went on to LBC radio and was asked to open an exhibition at a museum. I was even asked to retire my crystal stick and the clothes that I wore to become exhibits at another museum, the Pump House, along with an Albin wall of memorabilia that tells the story of Albin's and the television programme, a fantastic honour. I was invited to speak at dinners. People from all over the country contacted us asking whether they could meet me as well as people from the company. It was overwhelming and very exciting.

One lovely lady came from Essex to meet me and to arrange her own and her husband's funerals for the future. The programme had that much of an impact on her, and she had made her mind up that no one else was going to do her funeral. She had even told Jackie that if we could not go to Essex, she would move to Bermondsey. What a wonderful compliment! As I walked into the room, fresh from a funeral with my hat, stick and gloves in my hand, she looked at me and said, 'Ah, there's the man. Oh, I did love your programme. I do think you are lovely. Would you mind if I touched your crystal knob?'

'Madam,' I replied, 'we've not even been introduced.'

We all laughed and she said, 'See, I knew you had a good sense of humour.'

Quite unbelievable was the lady who came from Norfolk.

Yes, Norfolk to Bermondsey. The girls invited her in for a cup of tea but she would not come in; she just wanted to wait outside. As I arrived back from a funeral and got out of the limousine, she came over to me and said, 'I think your programme was wonderful and you changed the whole way I feel about dying. I was afraid. I'm not afraid any more, but I'm going to ask you something and you are going to think I'm really silly.'

'No, please, what can I do?'

She replied, 'Could I touch your hair? I just want to touch your hair, I think it's lovely.'

I did not know what to say so I leaned gently forward and she timidly and softly touched my hair, thanked me sincerely, wished me a good life and left. You are probably thinking, 'No, surely not!' but, as God is my witness, that is exactly what happened.

Another lady, also from the Norwich area, had lost her brother, who lived in Edmonton, and asked for us to go across and conduct the funeral. Having seen the programme, all she wanted for her brother was for Albin's to be the funeral directors. This of course we agreed to, with my sons conducting. It was a horsedrawn funeral with three limousines, and this lady could not have been happier or more grateful with everything we did. She also came along to our Christmas memorial service and stayed afterwards for something to eat with us. She is a beautiful and kind lady, and I shall always remember her fondly for her gentle way.

I received approval from the local residents too. One of the waiters at our local La Lanterna restaurant had seen a picture of me on the back of a magazine someone was reading on the tube. There I was, in my black mourning suit, along with the word 'Dead', and he had thought, 'Ah, that's Mr Barry who comes to the restaurant. He must have died. Oh dear.'

So he went into the restaurant and told all the other waiters, the chef and the owner that I had died. But they knew better and told him, 'No, he's on the television programme,' so when Jackie and I turned up for a meal on the Saturday evening, there was a shout of 'See, he's alive!' I have had a lot of things written about me but never an obituary. At least the young waiter was pleased to see me alive – I must be a good tipper.

People in the area have been fantastic. In the local shops, they like to serve me quickly, and if I am walking along the street or pull up at the traffic lights, somebody will inevitably shout, 'Hey Barry, don't drop the coffin, mate.' I take it all in good fun as these are great people and this is just their way of being affectionate. Whenever I pass the minicab office at Dockhead, they often shout out, 'All right, Bal, loved the programme.' Now, next to the minicab office is a kebab restaurant that is being renovated. One day I made the mistake of asking the minicab drivers, as they sat outside, what the new restaurant was going to be called. 'They're going to name it after you, Bal – don't drop the kebab.' They really are a handful.

One lady sent us a beautiful letter along with a lottery ticket for £5 that she had bought for that Saturday's big rollover draw. She wanted any winnings to be shared between all the boys and girls at the firm, who she thought were lovely. It is probably fortunate for me that we did not win because I guess none of them would be at work now, and my family and I would be the only ones left at Albin's.

Even Perry, our young apprentice, achieved some fame. He is the one in the programme who had about three attempts at passing his driving theory test. Well, after that he went on and passed his driving test first time. Going to one funeral, Perry was driving the hearse with me in the passenger seat (that's how all new drivers begin to learn the skills of hearse-driving) and we were about to turn right into Pomeroy Street from the Old Kent Road. As we began our turn, 'white van man' zoomed up and swerved round the front of the hearse. Fortunately, two traffic policemen were waiting on motorbikes to turn out of Pomeroy Street into the Old Kent Road. As Perry passed, one looked across and said, 'Don't worry, Perry, we're on it' – and off they went after the van driver.

On another occasion, a wise-guy in a car that pulled up alongside us opened his window and said to Perry, 'Have you passed your driving test yet?' Perry, behind the wheel of the hearse, just smiled, looked at me puzzled and nodded with some dignity.

'That's it, Perry, just wave and smile,' I said.

Well, if he hadn't passed his test, he would hardly be driving a hearse, would he?

Even less helpful was a man who came all the way from Leeds and asked Joanna, our receptionist and funeral arranger, whether he could pre-arrange a funeral for himself, claiming he had seen the programme and wanted us to do his funeral when the time came. Jo, always the professional, sat with the man for about half an hour going through all the details of what sort of funeral he would like and then produced all the documentation, gold folder, card and so on, everything we have for a pre-arranged funeral. She presented it to him for him to read through. The man opened his briefcase, placed the folder inside, thanked Jo and simply said, 'You are all celebrities now; I just wanted a souvenir. Thanks a lot,' and left. Jo was understandably speechless – or, as we say in Bermondsey, 'gobsmacked'.

It is amazing the lengths that some people will go to, and the response to the programme has been a real eye-opener. Most other funeral directors accepted the programme in general very well, and our national association wrote and commended us on representing the profession so wonderfully well (which made me feel very proud). I replied to each and every communication that I received, which now amounts to thousands. Some wanted a signed photograph. Others wanted me to sign copies of the book that they had bought. Some just wanted to wish me well, and I honestly value each and every person.

What was most surprising to me was that people felt that the showing and success of the programme might make me change in some way: perhaps I would no longer be available to do their family funerals personally. But they need not worry. I am first and last a funeral director; that's what I do, and that's not going to change. All the recognition that has come with the programme has just been really nice, complimentary, stressful, but an incredible experience and one I really value.

With all those thousands of good wishes came only two complaints. No disrespect to Wales, but both emanated from there. One was from a funeral director who wrote complaining that, in the programme he had watched the previous day, where we carried a 26-stone man into church for a funeral service, I had deceived the public. He said that six people and myself could not carry a 26-stone man in a coffin, so the coffin must have been empty, the funeral either a ruse or very much against health and safety legislation. 'Surely this man cannot be serious?' I thought. As if I would lower myself to do anything like that.

But then I decided it was a bit of a compliment to our pall-bearers and to me. Everything seen in that television series actually happened. Nothing was set up or rigged, and there were certainly no tricks. The funeral was a genuine funeral, and the coffin was indeed carried by six strong, professional and experienced pall-bearers. As the hearse had a high bier, there was no major bending involved, and I was at the head of the coffin to steady it and take the weight. We carried the coffin into the church and on to tall trestles approximately the height of the hearse bier, no health and safety rules being broken at any point. There should be no change in one's professional etiquette just because somebody is large in size. We must do everything within our power to complete the funeral with the same amount of respect and dignity in every case, and I know my staff are completely behind me in that.

The second complaint was also from a funeral director in Wales, a far less gracious fellow who complained, 'Now then, I think it is terrible that you are eating breakfast before you go to do somebody's funeral. It's very disrespectful, I think, and as you are all leaving the firm to go home, my goodness, if you didn't have a snowball fight in front of the cameras now. Again very disrespectful is that. Now I ask you, don't you think you are doing the funeral profession a very ungracious service?'

At first, I honestly thought this was somebody pulling my leg rather than a genuine complaint, but when I realised that he was for real, I did not know whether to laugh or cry. As they are part of the same emotion, I doubt it would have made any difference which I did.

We are, it has to be remembered, not robots. Having a little fun with each other on the way home helps to keep everyone sane. After all, we do a very serious job all day long.

And why shouldn't we sit down and enjoy a meal together? Did this gentleman think that we perhaps don't need to eat? Eating together in the mornings is team-building, helpful and necessary to us all. When we walk out from breakfast and are ready to carry out our duty for the bereaved, the mood changes and we become very professional. Everything in its proper place. For me, the whole point of the programme was to show that we are human, just like everybody else. In life, we have to find a balance between our work and our social lives. Just because our work is sometimes sad, difficult and different from the normal everyday jobs that other people may have does not mean that we should never, ever be happy in what we do. No sir!

But I did not have to tell this gentleman that his perception was wrong – someone else did that for me. Amazingly, one of this funeral director's fellow countrymen had seen an article in which the funeral director, whose picture appeared in the text, had taken it upon himself to criticise our firm and the programme itself. This second fellow, whom I had never met, was outraged at the comments and went to see him face to face to tell him so. My defender then drove all the way from Wales to meet me personally, eventually spending most of the day here with us. He was an old fan of the programme, a very kind and interesting man who loved people and conversation. I just smiled at the article he showed me, usually the best way. I am sure the writer is a good man and probably a fine funeral director, but we will just have to agree to continue our work in different styles. If the whole world could do that, it would be a better place, don't you think? Let's just agree to differ.

One muted criticism came from yet another funeral director, the man concerned having already agreed that it was a very good programme but feeling that it was all possibly shown in too perfect a light. To him, nothing seemed to go wrong in the programme. Again, I took that as a compliment because, throughout the programme, things were going amiss! Problems confronted us and, as always, mistakes occurred, but it is how they were dealt with that made all the difference. The general public can be excused for not noticing them, but an experienced funeral director should have spotted the following (apologies here if you have not seen the episodes concerned):

1   Elaine from our Deptford office, outside the church at the West Indian funeral phoning the cemetery to tell them that we would be approximately an hour late as the service was overrunning.

2   Ben's large horsedrawn funeral at Hither Green entering the cemetery in darkness (we do not usually have funerals in the dark, you know) – we were obviously running *very* late.

3   The old gentleman who had been left at the church in his wheelchair after the Mass of one horsedrawn funeral. An ambulance was supposed to have collected the gentleman after the Mass, yet as we passed the church on the way back to the family pub, he was still there and I then anxiously tried to organise the ambulance and get him into the priest's house for warmth.

4   Traffic problems, the curse of every inner-city funeral director. My son Simon eloquently described some of the difficulties with bus lanes in the programme.

5   The number of flowers – very wet, some very flimsy – that faced us at Ben's funeral. The weather conditions were clearly causing problems.

6   The difficulties I had with time-keeping and absence with

Jamela, the trainee embalmer, ending with my calling her into the office to discipline her.

7 When we had to bump a car, badly parked outside the church in a narrow road, so that we could get the funeral cortège through.

8 My son Jonathan arriving at the address provided, only to find that the Iranian family had left the 'green certificate' – the permission slip for burial or cremation that is issued by the registrar – at another address. As the gentleman concerned turned to fly off in the car to try to retrieve it so that we could get to the cemetery on time, he said, 'Please don't worry, I have a very fast car.' Then came Jonathan's wonderful, quietly spoken reply: 'There's no such thing as a fast car in London, so please don't rush.'

9 Our behind-the-scenes panic at the Memorial Garden service as we were trying to blow up about a thousand balloons. As they were blowing away in the wind, I was screaming to the guys walking across the yard to 'Get those balloons inside!'

Nothing's ever perfect, but I hope we carried these challenges off with some dignity. Perhaps our critic was looking for problems such as staff being late, incorrectly dressed or unhappy, rudeness, poor leadership, unprofessional behaviour or bad organisation. In that case, he was looking at the wrong funeral firm because you will not find that at Albin's.

What the programme also did, which greatly pleased me, was awaken young people to the career possibilities within the industry. The number of young people who contacted me after the show wanting to be embalmers, the number who applied to do the diploma course, the number of communications I had from people who wanted to work here, all of them young, was astounding. I used to worry that we would never get young people to work in a profession such as this, but my fears seem to have been unfounded. I have around me a fantastic young team, and people are now seeing this work as a true calling and a good way to spend your life in the service of others.

There were other brilliant reactions too. Some viewers wanted Father Alan, 'Simba', who sang at the Memorial Garden service, to make a CD of crooning songs. Many people were amazed that Father Peter, a wonderfully sincere man, really did spend the night with the deceased in church. At the time, he himself said, 'People are going to think I am crazy but I don't care,' and he really doesn't. What he did I personally think was brave, comforting and lovely, spending the night protecting the soul and re-enacting how he had watched television with the deceased in her lifetime every week. You have got to admire someone like that. But, to me, the real stars were the people who volunteered to tell their stories on camera. They were fantastic and made the whole programme very special.

The programme is now being broadcast around the world – Australia, New Zealand, France, Poland and Holland, I believe. Holland has been the first country to broadcast *Don't Drop the Coffin* outside the UK. I have had some touching e-mails from people in Holland, including one from a young lady in the funeral profession who wants to spend two weeks working with us here in the summer. But perhaps the funniest e-mail I had came from a lady called Birgit Leerling, who was arranging the subtitles for Dutch television. Here are her e-mail, referring to the first episode, and my reply:

My name is Birgit Leerling, I am from Holland and I'm a subtitler for television. Currently I am working on episode 1 of a program called 'Don't drop the coffin', with which you are undoubtedly familiar. I am having problems with the spelling of a few names of your employees. I have a script, in which the following string of names is given: Pugh, Pugh, Bone in the Gru, Cuffbert, Devone and Grower. Could you please tell me whether these names are spelled correctly? I would be very grateful if I were to received a reply from you. Thanks in advance.

Dear Birgit,
Thank you for your enquiry concerning 'Don't Drop the Coffin'.
   I realise how difficult it must be trying to translate names that are not familiar to you. The names you hear on the programme are not in fact names of our employees, but names belonging to characters from an old children's programme which used to be shown on British TV some years ago. The children's programme was called 'Trumpton' and was based on a village fire fighters' station. During the programme, whenever the characters were called out to attend an emergency, the music played and the

'firemen' came out of the station as their names were read out. As I had jokingly made a reference to the Trumpton characters when talking to my staff, the television company thought it would be amusing to use the Trumpton music and names as the staff left the office.

As most people here remember fondly the Trumpton programme, our television viewers thought this was very amusing when shown on British TV. I am not sure that the same would happen in other countries unless Trumpton was familiar to you, but for your information the characters referred to were in fact Pugh, Pugh, Barney McGrew, Cuthbert, Dibble and Grubb.

Good luck with the programme and I do hope it is received well in Holland.

Head of Fire Station Trumpton
Chief Officer Barry

We all had a tremendous laugh over that.

When the series finished, a little inconclusively some people thought, there were still questions to be answered. People would stop and ask me what happened here and what happened there, so, just for your curiosity, yes, as I've already said, Perry did eventually pass his theory test. Interestingly enough, his young brother, almost his identical twin, is also now working as a young apprentice, so I now have the nightmare of a Perry clone, but they're good lads. No, Jamela didn't make it in the end but, at the opposite end of the scale, now has a recording contract and is, I have been told, singing in a band. No, Father Alan hasn't made a CD (not that I am aware of anyway).

Yes, all the doves did come back from that night's service. Yes, we do have breakfast every day, believe it or not, including a cooked one on Fridays. No, that's not our only uniform; you saw our winter coats as the programme was actually filmed through the winter, but we have light tails for the spring, summer and early autumn. Yes, we do have that kind of memorial service every year in early December. No, our cars are not all black – they are black and burgundy, in the royal colours. Yes, we do have our own doves that live in a dovecote on the edge of the Memorial Garden. Yes, the carriage and two horses – Fred and George – are ours. No, I don't often go round dressed as Austin Powers!

And the answer to the question that everyone seems to have been asking: we will just have to wait and see whether there will be another series, although this has been suggested. (And no, we were not paid a fortune – this was a documentary, not a drama series!) All in all, the series has been something I am sincerely proud of, and, in the last analysis, putting my head on the block was well worth it.

What you are about to read is a sincerely honest, unedited cross-section of letters and e-mails received from the general public and from funeral directors. I have chosen just a few of the many that arrived. The authors, whose names and addresses have been omitted for confidentiality, have agreed to their inclusion, and I have replied to every communication I have received. I am very proud of these letters and e-mails because, as I mentioned above, all bar two have been positive. It is often said that those who are successful are lucky, but it never ceases to amaze me that the harder you work, the luckier you seem to get.

In October 2001 I attended the funeral of
my sister-in-law, a lady who lived in
Bermondsey all her married life, but was
born and spent her youth in the far north
of Scotland. I had never attended a funeral
so far south before so was slightly apprehensive. I need not have been. From the
moment the funeral cortège entered the
square I was immediately engrossed with
the sheer dignity, sensitivity and compassion with which it was conducted. I was
in car no. 3, and shall always remember
what the young man said to me - he actually
spoke to me - I now wonder which of the
staff it was. I watched and drank it all
in. Barry calling out our names, the little
red carpets, his quiet authority, going in
front of the hearse with his cane, etc.,
etc. I keep it all in my memory bank. On
our way to the Cemetery I observed the car
number plates carried the firm's initials:
Barry coming back for a soft drink afterwards. How I wished I had the courage to
say thank you as he passed me by on his way
out.

Much later in 2002 my niece, who knew of
my admiration for F. A. Albin's, rang me
to say Barry has written a book, 'Don't
Drop the Coffin'. Needless to say she got
me a copy and had it signed by Barry. My
interest and respect grew as I read the
book. She has also sent me her programme
of your Christmas Service.

Now I've watched the television series.
I was not disappointed. It was good.

I've admired you 'from afar', Barry,
and your team of true professionals, but
most of all, which is so refreshing, you

have not forgotten your roots. Thank you again.

I'm not sure if you expected or have indeed received any letters as a result of your ITV series and book but I just felt compelled to write to you.

I found the TV series both informative and touching as many people, including myself, are often curious about death – your programmes managed to shed light on the profession without being morbid.

The approach you take to your job truly amazes me – you obviously have so much passion for your work and that shows in the funerals you conduct.

After being intrigued by the programme I decided to buy your book and thought it was just fantastic – I read it in 2 days! It gave me an even greater insight into your life and those of your staff. You must be so proud of your sons.

I totally agree with you about everybody being equal in death and the procedure you have put in place for the foetuses touched me so much. I think it is lovely that parents have somewhere to mourn their babies.

I myself have never actually attended a funeral of a loved one (but then I am only 21) but can only imagine how distressing it can be. From reading your book you and your staff go to great lengths to make the whole process, from instructing you to the final details, a lot easier for the grieving family.

You have obviously carried on the Albin tradition in true form. It is obvious that from your hard work you have made a great name for yourself in

Bermondsey – and a lasting impression on me. I
know I will read your book again and really this was
just a note to say that you should be so proud of
yourself and your workforce. If I can say all this
without having met you then the praise you get off
those who have must be immense.

Thank you for taking the time to read my letter. If
you are not too busy it would be nice to hear back
from you – if anything, just to know you have
received the letter.

I felt compelled to write to you after
seeing last night's episode of 'Don't Drop
the Coffin'. I would like to compliment
you and your team for the job you do, and
the professional way you all seem to be
able to conduct yourselves.

Over the past two years I have had many
dealings with undertakers; in March 2002
my wife was murdered in East London, and I
had to deal with so many issues arising
from that, and in June this year my Mother
passed on, and I am still coming to terms
with that loss.

I have watched the programme featuring
your company and although I do realise
that it is a business, the way you conduct
yourselves is commendable. Although I have
shed many tears watching the programme,
especially last night's edition, I was so
impressed that you give me back so much,
and care about what you do, with such
feeling.

I thank you all for giving people like
myself some comfort and insight into how
things are done, and helping us cope.

* * *

I come from Poland. Seven days ago I have watched a film in TV about you and your funeral company.

I was 'charmed' by your personality and your attitude to work in this specific profession. I work in this profession too. I am the owner of three funeral houses (one in the capital city – Warsaw). I also have a 'coffin factory'.

Dear Mr Barry, I would be very pleased to get to know you and your company. I would also like to invite you to Poland. I think this could be a new experience for you. As I saw you are very interested in what is going on in the funeral business for you. I am interested in this too. Sometimes I go out on funeral markets to Germany, France, Belgium and Italy, I would visit English markets with pleasure.

I also keep contacts with undertakers from UE [European Union] countries. I think it is very important, especially now when the degradation of spiritual values and degradation for 'dead people' continues. When I watched you and your company in TV I was pleased that you put so much attention to those things (respect and spiritual values). My personal way of this is very close to yours, you represent an unconventional approach of managing funeral company. That's why I would like to meet you very much.

Where do I start? I have watched 'Don't Drop the Coffin' every Tuesday riveted to my seat.

This has been the best documentary I have <u>ever</u> seen. I've cried every time too.

But I love it. Time stands still at 8.30–9.00.

You all have got such big hearts, caring and honest.

I've lost many loved ones, and always wondered what does happen behind the scenes. If it's like what you have shown, I'm at rest with myself now. Thank you so much.

Last night I saw what you do at Christmas. Please Mr Albin, may I have a ticket reserved for me to come this year and buy a star, and balloon for my Dear Mum and Son? I'd like to be there on that special night. It would be the best Christmas present I could ever have. My cancer treatment will be easier to face.
Thank you for reading this.

Now that I have found your web site, I felt I had to write to you to let you know how your programme has helped me because of the insight it provided. I am only 41 and hopefully have a long time yet, but it prompted me to think about the future. I made a will last week – something I have been putting off for years.

I lost both my parents within 6 weeks 12 years ago, which took a lot of getting over. Not sure I am there yet, or if I ever will be. When they died I was in a state of shock and remember very little about the funeral. I found both cremations profoundly shocking and what I am trying to say is that your series of programmes has helped me. I suppose some of the mystery and fear has gone.

I think you all do a wonderful job and you all

58

clearly care. I cried my eyes out when I watched the Memorial Garden programme – a truly wonderful place and event to hold.

Please pass on my thoughts if you have time during one of your breakfast meetings.

I just wanted to say what a fascinating programme Don't Drop the Coffin was. I very recently lost my Mother and thought I would be unable to watch your programme but it actually went some way to helping me come to terms with my loss. You were all so caring and friendly – it's a pity the last of the series was screened tonight – I shall miss my weekly visit to Albins. Keep up the excellent, caring and very important work you all do.

I enjoyed the program this evening. On two levels. Having lost my wife last year who worked with me in the trade. But mostly as a retired funeral director, you and all of the members of your staff did us proud. It ain't easy at home alone, I shed a tear.

Thank you.

You may think this is a very strange thing to say, but I feel I wish to convey to you this statement. Until watching your program I had a real fear of dying. All my family know this. However your programme has really put me at rest now.

I know, as I live in Essex, I could never be looked after by your wonderful staff, when my time comes. However I will search out a director who will take as much care as your family does to see me when the time is right.

May I thank you and your staff for helping me overcome this mortal fear?

Just read your second book. It was great, will you be writing another one?

It has made me want to be a funeral director even more now and it is easier in a way to deal with death. I read the book within a week, I was driving my husband mad with it. Some stories were funny and some very sad but people deal with death in different ways. Please don't give up writing, you have so much to share with other people and hopefully you will make another programme. Keep up the good work, take care.

I visited your website after watching the Documentary that was screened recently on TV. The Documentary was watched by my husband and myself and was found to be very interesting. We have lost two of our precious Baby Sons . . . We found out at the 20 week routine ultrasound scans that they had a condition known as 'ARPKD' (Autosomal Recessive Polycystic Kidney Disease), better known as 'Potters Syndrome' . . . – was born on November 27th 2000 and lived for just 5 very short minutes after his birth before he passed to Heaven, and our – was born on February 26th 2002 and lived for just 30 very short minutes before he passed to Heaven too . . .

We found out at both of their 20 week routine pregnancy ultrasound scans that they had this syndrome (usually fatal at birth, but no problems during the 9 months of pregnancy) . . . We carried to full term, both times, hoping and praying for a miracle, heartbreakingly our miracles never came, and both our babies now rest peacefully together, in Heaven . . . We were able to have a home birth with our second Potters Baby —, (— was breech so had to be born in hospital), but we kept our babies at home with us for a few days after they had passed, and then brought them home again the day before their funeral days, so that we could spend another whole night with our angels, before that final goodbye . . . We had their Funerals carried out with them both in their Moses Baskets, so we were able to feel and touch and hold our babies throughout the Services . . . My husband and I carried our babies to the Church and to the Crematorium both times and when the time came, I laid my little angels in their tiny caskets that we had made for them, which was the final straw that truly broke our hearts: We have two older children born previous to our Potters Babies, — 13 and — 5, and we always do something special in their memories at special times of the year . . . This brings me to my question that I am writing to you about . . . Can you please let me know if you have had your Memorial/ Remembrance day/evening that you arrange in memory of all those who have lost someone they love . . . We watched this on your TV Documentary, and would like to know if you are having one this year or if it has passed already . . . We live in Essex, but would so like to come and join in this with everyone, if it has not already passed? I will leave here the website that I made in memory of our two little angels, in case you may ever wish to visit . . . Again, thank you for allowing the cameras into your life and your work to allow others, like us, who have lost babies/children/loved ones in their lives, to try and come to terms a little more with the way things are carried out when our loved ones pass . . . I hope to hear back from you soon, and hope that we have not missed your Remembrance Day for this year.

I've been watching your Television series of Don't Drop the Coffin, and I've read your book. I lost my Father to Suicide, 10 yrs October 23rd; by watching your series and reading your book it's made me understand what happened to him before and after the funeral. I miss him dearly and would do anything to go back and stop him from his suicide. So I just like to say Thank you and Well done and good luck for the future of Albin and sons. It's helped me to understand death more so I'm not so scared.

THANX

Well, I cannot believe it was end of the best programme on TV; Barry can I buy the programmes on DVD, I have had a friend from Australia here with me and she would like a DVD as well. You have helped her face the death of a friend she helped nurse, that passed away last week, and the funeral is tomorrow. I went with her to the chapel of rest, to say my good byes.

How about that priest that sang at your remembrance service, you could do a Music CD, and the money goes to your favourite charities; I am first in line, for one of them and two DVDs. Tuesday night will never be the same, are you doing another one, looking forward to seeing it. How has the young girl got on doing the embalming, is she doing well? I hope we can keep in touch now and again. All the best to all at Albins, lets hope more on TV. God Bless and keep up the good work.

I watched the recent 'Don't Drop the Coffin' series on TV and just wanted to drop you a line. I'm not from around your area – Telford in Shropshire. I am 30 years old and have sadly lost both my parents to cancer, dad when I was 17 and mom when I was 23. I have always had a kind of 'phobia' about funerals/ funeral directors etc. which stemmed from going to see my dad in the chapel of rest – a memory which has always haunted me. I had nothing to do with the funeral arrangements and the 'ignorance is bliss' did not help with my grieving. Your programme gave me a great deal of comfort, your company is totally professional and the staff are dedicated and just brilliant – you obviously give so much comfort to many people in their time of need. It certainly made me think about the work that goes on behind the scenes when someone dies – I can only hope that the people who dealt with my parents were somewhere in your league. Thank you for making me laugh, cry and be comforted.

* * *

I just had to write and say how much I am enjoying your T.V. programme. It is so good to watch the goings on amongst you all; it must be very hard for you all at times, but I love to see the fun you have among yourselves, you could not do the job without it. I expected it to be a sad and serious programme, but I have shed some tears and had some good laughs along with you all. I lost my mum in January this year, I wish I had seen the programme before it happened, as I was so frightened of death, but now I am seeing it in a different light thanks to you all. I enjoyed the Dove and Carol service that was on tonight; if you have another one this year could you let me know the date as I would love to attend. Thanks once again for a most interesting and funny programme, looking forward to next weeks. Best Wishes to all.

Read the book and watched every episode so far, had to write and congratulate you on a heart warming and yet informative book and likewise a fascinating series. Having lost both my parents I have encouraged my youngest son (14) to sit and watch your programme with me, in a hope that he will learn to accept death as a new beginning and not a thing to fear. Once again congratulations to both you and your staff.

Just wanted to say thanks for the programme. In a strange way it's been a bit of a comfort recently as my three grand-parents are all suffering the effects of old age, strokes, nursing homes etc and you can't get away from the fact that we will have to deal with their passing away in the near future. Very upsetting as we are a very close family but I think it is the human touch you put on whole process and the obvious care you have for others that is helping me cope. Also, Granddad is a Bermondsey boy born and bred and it's good to hear South East London accents on the TV!

Thanks again and keep up the good work.

Barry,

I hope you will forgive me sending you yet another e-mail, but I have just finished reading your wonderful book 'Final Departures', and I wanted to tell you not only how much I enjoyed it, but how it has helped me personally deal with my own recent loss.

As ever, the tales in the book were handled with your usual sense of respect and good natured humour, and while you – quite rightly in some cases – poked a little fun at some of the more 'unusual' aspects of death and funerals, I never felt you were attempting to take cheap shots. Your respect for people's right to decide, and your general approach that we are all equal in the end, comes through once again in this book, just as it does in your other book, and indeed in dealing with you in person.

Now, as far as the book helped me. You might recall that we lost my Nan in February, and your firm conducted the funeral for us on March 8th. A mere three days later, I was due to take my Mum to New York for a trip we had had planned for over a year. As it turned out, the timing was actually very good as it gave her a chance to get away and clear her head. We had a great time.

Now, much as I think you are yourself, I have always been a big fan of the States. I've studied American history, and I've made quite a few trips there. The events of September 11th 2001 affected me quite deeply, especially as I was actually due to be in New York just weeks after the incident. I had cancelled that trip at the time, and this was my first chance to go back. Mum and I had decided when we organised this trip that we had to go to Ground Zero, and the memorial in Battery Park, and pay our respects. Now, after the funeral, it somehow seemed even more important.

As you know, it's an emotional place to be, and we both shed a few tears as we looked over the site, and memories of the lost lives mingled with our own still raw emotions. But I also think it helped us get a sense of perspective, and to deal with the loss. Seeing how New York has recovered since that awful day made us think that we could likewise deal with this. Like the city, it would never be the same, but it didn't have to be.

Now, a little over a month after our return, I read your book, and I read your comments about the way the US nation dealt with the aftermath of 9/11. Your comments on comparing that great loss with the individual feelings of grief we feel when we lose someone. Somehow those words just brought it all together for me, they helped close the circle, and as soon as I finished the book I immediately felt better. I understood now why I needed to go there and why I had felt as I had. I understood how it had helped me. Those words helped me more than my week of introspective brooding had done.

So thank you, Barry. I can't really say a lot more than that. Thank you.

I sincerely hope that you have enjoyed reading these letters and e-mails as much as I have enjoyed receiving them. They are all a true inspiration to continue one's work.

One of my proudest achievements is that, finally, after many years of trying, one of our local Catholic schools has asked me to speak to children aged 9½ to 11½ about the celebration of death within funerals, how to cope and how to begin to understand why we have funerals. This is a real milestone because, with all our help and with an openness to dealing with death, which must include our children, we will help to remove the stigma and fear, referred to in several of the letters above, for future generations.

4

RETURN TO THE STATES

Anyone who has visited some of America's more colourful cemeteries might be forgiven for thinking that they are a little like Disneyland without any exits. It is the American culture, it seems, to present everything right 'in your face', and the funeral industry is no exception.

Having said that, America is probably the only other place in the world where I could ever consider living or working, particularly in my line of work. The funeral industry in America is certainly a benchmark for every other country to follow. It demands the highest qualifications and standards. Every funeral director in the US has to qualify through a funeral college to be a licensed funeral director; in order to keep that licence once it has been issued, they must then undergo continuous accredited education. Failing to do this, or breaching any of the industry's rules or standards, will result in heavy fines or revocation of the state licence, leaving the funeral director unable to operate – in every state, that is, but Colorado. The powers that be in Colorado have decided not to have rigid licensing rules but to treat funeral directing much like any other business trading in the state, yet I am told that you cannot find one funeral director in Colorado who does not hold a licence. So strong is the funeral lobby that no one dares employ an unlicensed person even though licensing is not necessary.

On my many visits to the US, I have enjoyed many of the benefits of their education over my lifetime. I have attended many lectures and even given a few. I have helped my dear friend Carole Bearden through her state licence exams. Wherever I have travelled, I have taken the time to educate myself in local funeral practices. I have also learned many of the trade secrets of embalming from attending so many of the exhibition courses that they hold at their regular seminars, so, all in all, it is clear that I owe much of my educational knowledge of funeral directing and embalming to the US. Along the way, I have made countless friends. I am also *immensely* proud to be the only English funeral director to have received a Doctorate of Humane Letters – honoris causa – from the world-renowned, number one college for funeral directing in the world, the Commonwealth Institute in Houston, Texas. So it is Dr Barry now – not that the girls at the office will let me examine them!

In early November 2003, the college flew Jackie and myself to Houston, where they held a dinner in my honour. It was a little like one of those evenings you sometimes see on television when friends and colleagues spend the whole evening publicly saying nice things about a particular person. The professors and tutors of the college knew my track record well and were, throughout the dinner, embarrassingly and unashamedly exactly what you might expect in the US. You've got it – right in your face. Yet their kindness, manners and generosity were also very American – second to none. They were fantastic; so overwhelming was their kindness that it left Jackie and Carol in tears.

The next morning I was taken to a huge auditorium where I was to speak, as my old friend and president of the college, Todd Van Beck, had instructed me, for as long as I wanted about whatever I wanted for the new graduates who were all receiving the diplomas that would enable them to obtain licences. I'm never one to miss an opportunity to jump on a soap box, but there was one catch – whatever I said or whatever I did, I definitely had to inspire them. OK, I thought.

I started with, 'Right, sit up straight, fold your arms and face the front!' quite loudly and in a very strict tone. Their faces were a picture. Some did even fold their arms and sit up straight, exactly as I had demanded.

I paused, watched and continued in a gentler voice, 'No, relax please. I'm only kidding. It's just that I have always wanted to say that to a hall full of attentive students. So there you are. I haven't started but you have fulfilled one of the things I most wanted to do before I die.'

The audience immediately relaxed and laughed. We were friends, and I had got off to a good start. Throughout my twenty- or twenty-five-minute speech, we shared much laughter as well as, I hope, a reasonable amount of inspiration and definitely some major principles to take them through their careers as funeral directors.

At the end of the speech, with Jackie and Carol still in tears, I received a standing ovation and a lot of American-style yelping from the students, their families and the tutors and professors behind me on the stage. I couldn't help thinking of an old statement once made by Samuel Goldwin. He once said, at the end of a major achievement, 'If I could die now, I would be the happiest man alive.' Todd followed my speech with a big thank-you and a long list of reasons why I was receiving this honour. Then I was presented with the honorary doctorate for having achieved the 'most highest of standards in a lifetime career' (his words, not mine). He believed that this was the first to be awarded within the funeral industry for the study of bereavement, funeral practice, the history of the service and embalming principles, also taking into account my work as an author to the profession, and my courage and success with the media through the television series *Don't Drop the Coffin*. I was gobsmacked, as we say in Bermondsey.

Everybody stood as I received the degree. It was a moment of great emotion, but the best was still to come. I was then dressed in a gown and honoured for the presentation with the robes of a Doctor of Letters, all turquoise, lemon and lilac. By now I was overwhelmed, my heart was pounding and there was a lump in my throat. Ringing through my head was one of the mottoes that has taken me through my life as a funeral director when dealing with the bereaved: 'It is already bad enough; don't make it any worse.' This was closely followed by, 'It can't get any better today; please don't make it any worse.'

The graduation degrees were then issued to the students and we were all taken back to the main building of the Commonwealth Institute, which houses probably the greatest funeral museum in the world. There were Buick hearses from times past. Relics from the funerals of Abraham Lincoln and Elvis Presley. Some of the first embalming tables and tools ever used. Old coffins, and early iceboxes which were used to preserve corpses. There were many old funeral uniforms. Photographs. Horsedrawn coaches. A whole section on the funerals of the Kennedy family and other presidents. For someone like me, it was like being Peter Pan in Neverland. I could have stayed there all day, but there was food to eat and people to talk to. It all came to an end far too soon. As I lay in bed that evening, reliving the day's events, I thought of my sons holding the fort back in the UK and how their existence makes everything I have done or will do worthwhile. Albin's will live on. Right now was my moment, but theirs was yet to come.

Moments later I drifted off to sleep – the end of a perfect day. I had given every student a memento from F.A. Albin & Sons, the tutors and professors receiving copies of my book *Don't Drop the Coffin* (signed, of course!). The thought crossed my mind that, with my doctorate degree, I was probably now a fully fledged honorary American funeral director too, which Todd assured me I was.

I had been in the States earlier that year completing the last programme in the series of *Don't Drop the Coffin*, which had been a fantastic experience. We had visited the Cryonics Institute in Detroit for the first part of the programme and then flew down to an exhibition of funeral memorialisation in Las Vegas, where, for the first time in my life, I was allowed to do a little presenting and had the great privilege of interviewing Todd, my friend for sixteen years and the president of the Commonwealth Institute. He is in my opinion the leading light in the world of funeral directing, a man who has my highest respect and admiration.

Todd gave me an amazing interview in which he feared somewhat for the American funeral itself and lamented the fact that everything seemed to be done with speed. He said, 'Here we have what I call the McFuneral. You see, you can get a McDonald's in three minutes or a McFuneral in three hours and neither are good for you.' Here he was referring to cremations, which are carried out very differently in America. They are often completed swiftly and without a service, usually in nothing more than a cardboard case. As such, cremation is to some degree unregulated in America, which is quite the opposite of the situation in the UK. It is strange that funeral directors in America are highly regulated whereas those in the UK are not regulated at all, yet cremation in the UK is highly regulated and cremation in America is hardly regulated at all. Something not quite right there. Todd's was definitely the best interview I have ever been involved in, but it will not be shown until a later series – if, of course, we have one.

You might have seen me in *Don't Drop the Coffin* going on to play the great Austin Powers with my exquisite false teeth, Roy Orbison glasses, blue velvet suit and winkle-pickers. A possible Oscar-winning role? Modesty prevents me making a judgement, but the stark reality is that I obviously cannot act at all. So why did I do it in the first place? I too have been asking myself that. In actual fact, it was the television crew who talked me into it. Greatest responsibility lies with Debbie, one of the directors, who caused so many of the Austin Powers sequences to be cut because she could not stop laughing. I'll get my own back on her one day. However bad the acting, it at least showed that I could be a bit normal, if indeed anyone who dresses up as Austin Powers can be described as normal. It helped to introduce a lighter note at the end of a series about the serious subject of death and funeral directing and, I hope, left a smile on the faces of many who watched.

Some of the stories that come from the American funeral industry are quite incredible. A colleague told me of a guy in Ohio, aged forty-one, who had had a car accident and was recovering in hospital from a leg amputation. Imagine his reaction when he received a bill for $2,600 for the burial of the leg. At least the price included the cost of the plot, grave-diggers, minister and hearse. At the bottom of the invoice was a note saying that there would be an additional charge of $800 if the gentleman would like a headstone for his interred limb. I am even more surprised at this bill as American funeral directors usually remain debt free by asking for payment before anything takes place. Thank God we are not quite so direct in the UK.

One American funeral director with some TV fame, but of a very different kind from mine, is Carlo Constantino, the inspiration, so it is said, for the television series *The Sopranos*. Back in the 1920s and 1930s, Carlo is reputed to have designed and built double-decker coffins to hide murder victims, placing the bodies of those the Mafia had killed below those of his clients. Six pall-bearers carrying such a coffin must have struggled beyond all belief, assuming that the bodies were still in one piece. Much of this past was revealed in statements from a man called Anthony Rotondo when confessing to two murders he had himself committed, just a couple of the reputedly hundreds of Mafia murders back in that era.

Carlo's highly respected son Carl still manages a very successful, law-abiding funeral home in New Jersey, and it has been reported that Carlo himself even received a con-gratulatory telegram from President Bill Clinton on his hundredth birthday. It still sounds very frightening, and I'm very pleased to say that the only double-deckers in Bermondsey are red buses rather than coffins.

Now, we know that the act of dying in itself is easy. It's living that is the real trick; that is much harder. But even though I think we all recognise that, the fear of death itself is always with us. An amusing funeral director I met in Las Vegas said to me, 'Hey man, I'll know I'm dead when the mobile stops ringing.' (I wonder what he did before mobile phones?) I sincerely hope that he does not take calls during funeral services. That would be very unprofessional, but then we were in Las Vegas, where everything is larger than life – and death.

This man also told me his own motto: 'Do you know, Barry, what my aim is with the deceased? Well, if we can make the dead look better than you feel yourself, then man, we're doing a good job.' I didn't know whether to laugh or cry. For me, every deceased person I see reminds me how lucky I am to be alive. No matter how dreadful I feel, at least I am alive to feel it.

In Las Vegas, where this colleague was from, they specialise in what they call 'theme funerals'. The funeral home that this particular guy works for offers funerals with large backdrops of giant playing cards, huge dice and gigantic slot machines, all accompanied by a suitable casket to match. Above the backdrops and the caskets you can have, in flashing lights, the Las Vegas sign, with two enormous chips standing at each end of the casket. In fact, there is a whole brochure the bereaved can flick through to make their own personal gambling choice. You can design your own casket, with dice sewn inside the cover of the lid and playing cards embroidered on the inner silk. What next? Will people be giving the eulogy from a blackjack table? These funeral directors obviously see life as a bit of a crapshoot and are even prepared to make you a gravestone in any design you like. The most popular, amusingly, is a gigantic slot machine – although not my cup of tea – so you can have your last spin on life, I guess. To me, the only good thing for the deceased is that there would be no chance of paying out if someone had a lucky spin.

Another example of the American way of looking at things differently is that of a sixty-year-old man who was visiting a funeral home to pay his last respects to one of his colleagues. He took a wrong doorway, into an area he should incidentally not have been in, lost his footing on some stairs, fell and unfortunately broke his neck and died. The family unsuccessfully sued the funeral director but then, amazingly, insisted he undertook their funeral arrangements. They had a very interesting explanation for this: 'The suing was only business and not personal, and this is the best funeral home for miles so that's where Dad's going to be buried.' Nothing personal.

If anything is deliberate in America, though, it's the advertising. One of the worst advertisements I have ever seen in my life was an advert for term life insurance in an American daily newspaper. It had on it the company's logo, telephone numbers and all the usual 'You'll be surprised at how much you can afford – call for a quote' statements, but what was pretty shocking was that it included a photograph of the feet of a deceased person, complete with toe tag, lying uncovered on a slab. On the toe tag it said, 'The IRS [the American tax collection service] isn't calling you anymore' and at the bottom, 'Now they are calling your wife.' How cruel is that? What kind of mind works in such a fashion? Who would be moved to ring and buy insurance from such an advert? Not me, that's for sure!

In some ways, of course, the funeral industry is like any other in its trade magazines. There is regular advertising for funeral clothing, gravestone insurance and various types of coffin and casket, from willow baskets to elaborate American gold-plated caskets. Memorialisation from gravestones to small battery lights to put on memorials. Plaque photographs of the person you have loved and lost. Some even humorously run off the back of such television programmes as *Six Feet Under*, the top-rating American series about the Fisher Funeral Home. One company selling administration solutions for funeral directors starts its advert 'Are you six feet under with paperwork? Let us help you – we can dig you out of the hole you are in.' But that is for the trade press or usually seen only by other funeral directors. In America, you will see billboards for funeral services, memorialisation and cemetery parks as you drive along the freeway. There are television adverts for pre-paid funerals, similar ones appearing in national newspapers and of course on the radio. It seems that almost anything goes.

It is, however, all very different in the UK. There is very little funeral advertising in UK newspapers or on radio, and almost none at all on television, with the exception of a few adverts for life insurance policies. You might, in a daily newspaper, see an advert for a memorialisation company or a funeral director giving you his number should you want his professional services, but that is really where it ends. Apart from the recent advertising posters for *Six Feet Under*, which caused a stir. These soon had to be taken down when they fell foul of the UK Advertising Standards Authority, which instantly banned the posters after receiving a large number of complaints.

The posters had featured what appeared to be corpses advertising funeral products such as embalming fluid and wound filler, with ridiculous punch lines like 'Skin to die for'. I myself picked a similar leaflet out of a Sunday magazine introducing the Fisher and Sons Funeral Home (the funeral home from *Six Feet Under*) luxury range of long-lasting afterlife beauty accessories. There were three colourful bottles, like perfume bottles. On one was 'In Eternum + Wound Filler'. The second bottle had 'In Eternum + Embalming Fluid', and the third 'In Eternum + Lip Lock'. The reverse read, disgustingly, 'Banish unsightly blemishes caused by exposure to car crashes, stab wounds and other violent causes of death. In Eternum + Wound Filler helps return damaged skin to its previous perfect condition. This smooth flesh coloured cream is specially formulated to give the appearance of actual living tissue. The perfect solution to those funeral day dilemmas.' I, like many other people, thought that this was absolutely appalling. Whoever thought this up wants it used on them.

The whole unnecessary campaign was, thank goodness, banned. But such is the power of advertising that I had several phone calls asking whether these were real products. I suppose the end effect – which was what the television company desired – was that the people who saw the advertising had a shock and probably went on to watch the programme. This was a very unfortunate campaign as the series does not, in all honesty, reflect that advertisement in any way. It is well worth watching.

When I first went to America, I was shocked by some of the advertising that appeared in the funeral directories – the blue book, yellow book and red book – which are a little similar to our *Yellow Pages* but meant for funeral directors. In these, you would see such adverts as 'The only black funeral home in the area', 'The only Hispanic funeral home in the area' and, of course, 'The only white funeral home'. What really shocked me was that these advertisements were legal and seemed to be quite acceptable to all concerned. That was some twenty years ago, and things have now, at least outwardly, moved on. Having said that, what the funeral homes do now is to print pictures of the staff alongside the advertisements, instantly depicting what kind of funeral home it is. I truly believe that there will always be differences between people, races, traditions, customs and of course religions, and we all have to learn to live respectfully and peacefully with that without any form of victimisation. In the final analysis, we are all equal. All of us came into this world, and it is certain we will all leave it. Tolerance, compassion and respect are the only acceptable solutions to the problems we all create. I feel it is truly better that, as in the UK, our directories should reflect only the names of the funeral homes and a list of services they offer.

As I have just mentioned, I have visited America many times, and when I visit exhibitions I always bring something new back. Over the years I have brought back a piano organ that plays itself, a grave canopy to cover people in the wet, chair covers with 'Albin' on, jewellery that holds little specks of ashes, and flags that go on the bonnets of cars following funerals so that they do not get lost (very successful, these are, too).

This year I came back with some really interesting new products. For instance, floating biodegradable ashes boats. These are round discs, a bit like flying saucers, with a dent in the centre where you place the ashes. This is then sealed by an identical top depicting the person's favourite things in life – flowers, or somebody playing golf or soccer. Whatever you wanted can be painted on, or it can of course be left plain. You then seal the edges and float the boat into the water or the sea, perhaps with some flowers around it. In about ten minutes it disintegrates and the ashes spread on to the water. After it featured on our television programme *Don't Drop the*

Coffin, I received many phone calls from funeral directors and clients wanting to obtain some. Naturally, through my good friends Batesville – the biggest casket company in the world, the Nike of casket-making – I have been able to bring some to the UK.

There is also the casket with a little drawer in which you can place letters or people's own jewellery so that it can remain with them – simple but quite brilliant. Another product is 'Plant a heart and watch it grow'. This is a little heart made of a kind of rice paper into which seeds are sown. You can plant one in memory of somebody you have lost. The seeds grow within a few weeks, a constant reminder of your loved one. You can also bury a 'time capsule', a sealed chrome tube into which you can place any kind of memorabilia about the person who has died and bury it for somebody to find in the future. Products like these give people the freedom of choice they need in such situations. In this way, at least, America is several years in front of us with its good ideas.

Ending this chapter where we began – with Disney – the mind boggles at some of the ideas that may come next. Just when you thought there was nowhere left for the Disney Empire to spread to, the family has revealed its latest acquisition, a Californian cremation business called Neptune that has been purchased by Roy P. Disney, son of Walt Disney's Vice Chairman Roy E. Disney. Disney has reputedly bought Neptune for $11.5 million, also picking up some of the debts previously run up by the company. So what will we see now? Donald Duck handles on the urns? Mickey Mouse memorials? I dread to think.

But we still love you, America, really we do. You have been our greatest ally, and rumour has it that former Prime Minister Harold Wilson even seriously looked into making Britain a

legal state of America. And who knows what the future will
hold? Whatever happens, I will still be coming over every
year to see what is new in the States. What I can assure you,
however, is that Britain will never see a fast-funeral
'McAlbin's'. Trust me!

5

NOT FOR THE SQUEAMISH

Some of the responsibilities we undertake as funeral directors bring a whole mixture of emotions – laughter, tears, sadness, pride – but for me the most important word of all is 'responsibility'. If you choose to enter this profession, beware, because without showing responsibility you can never succeed. However gruesome the situation, however odd the request, however squeamish you may feel, there is no room for manoeuvre. Letting people down is not an option.

Luckily, some situations are peculiar rather than stomach-churning. A sweet old lady once asked me whether I would be kind enough to call her on the phone or call in to her house from time to time just to make sure she was still alive. She had recently lost her husband and really had nobody left in her life to keep an eye on her; her greatest fear was dying alone and being there for some time undiscovered. The fact that she trusted me enough professionally to accept the responsibility of that duty meant an awful lot to me, and of course even more to her. At the time she was in very good health physically but was obviously missing her husband greatly. I promised I would do exactly as she asked me, although I was sure that she would live for a long time to come without this worry to dwell on. She often made me a cake to say thank you, a lovely gesture. Wouldn't the world be a better place if we all did more of this? So I would call her every Friday morning, and if possible drop round to see her every few weeks. Over the next few months, we became quite good friends. Then, early one morning, I received a phone call from her GP to tell me that she had been rushed into hospital with pneumonia. A week later, she passed away. We undertook the funeral service and cremation, placing her ashes, laced together with her husband's, in our Memorial Garden. It's strange, isn't it? I had not been keeping an eye on her for very long but I missed ringing on a Friday. What had started as a kindness to her had, in a strange way, become a kindness to me.

Although I couldn't do this for everyone, I have since then taken on the same responsibility for two other elderly ladies who, I am glad to say (and I do mean that), are alive and well. One answers my calls with, 'No, Barry, don't you rub your hands together yet, I'm still alive, boy.'

'Elsie,' I reply, 'imagine we're having a game of snooker, love [she is a great fan of the snooker on the television so she knows exactly what I am talking about]. You place one of your balls right across the pocket, preventing me from putting any of my balls down. That's just where I want you – right on the edge of the pocket where I know you are mine – but I don't want you potted right until the end.'

'Oh well,' she'll say, 'I am well and truly snookered, ain't I, boy?'

The other dear old lady is totally different. Very serious, kind, clever, a little afraid and lonely in her life, she finds some security in the little dependence that she has on me. Just knowing I am there if she wants me is enough for her. And I'm glad I've been able to help in this instance.

As we get older, being alone becomes very frightening, and the smallest kindness shown is of great value. I am truly passionate about this aspect of my work. It can be difficult to draw a line and spread your time evenly, because if you cannot help someone without hurting someone else it is better not to try to help anybody. You must judge the balance correctly, because if people become too dependent on you and you on them it can cause great problems.

One lovely Bermondsey character comes around to see us at Albin's every week. Micky is about my age and I have known him since I was a young man, when he used to push a pram around Bermondsey collecting old newspaper and scrap to raise money. All the local kids knew him and would call out to him. He is not the full ticket but is, in his own way, happy, even though he can on occasions be very temperamental and difficult to handle. Sometimes he has been teased or misunderstood, but he likes me and always calls me Bawie. Micky lives with his family who look after him very well, but he likes just to walk around the whole of Bermondsey all day in all weathers – I don't think they can keep him in even if they want to. He pays me a visit every week, and I always give him something. Sometimes he stays for a cup of tea, and he will never leave until he has seen me. Nearly every month he will bring in a birthday card and try to convince me it is his birthday. Or he will bring in some old flowers someone has given him for the girls. When he was quite ill a couple of years ago with a stomach problem, I visited him in hospital. Delighted, he told everyone in the ward 'Bawie's come to see me.'

Sometimes, however, his visits are not at the best of times.

Lee once asked Micky to leave the courtyard as we were picking up a funeral. Micky kept saying, 'Where's Bawie, I've got to see Bawie,' but Lee was quite firm. To assist him Lee took him by the arm, but Micky swung a right-hander at him, only just missing him, and had to be calmed down and helped away. Not an easy task. Then he told his sister that we had hit him and she phoned me up just to check that he was okay and work out what had happened. She is a really nice lady. The next week, Micky was back again, looking for me and cracking a little joke about me: 'The pig goes oink oink, the cow goes moo, Bawie goes oh my God,' putting his hand up to his forehead and leaving us all in stitches. He of course said sorry to Lee, but that's another fight Lee has lost, bless him!

Kindness can sometimes, however, be misunderstood, as happened with my longest-serving member of staff, Reggie, who has been with me for about fifteen or sixteen years. Another real local character, Reg is an amazing driver who can drive day after day: Scotland, Cornwall, wherever you send him he loves a long journey. He was recently quite ill with a circulatory problem and taken into hospital for an important operation to replace a vein in his leg. As he was rushed into hospital, his wife Jill phoned Elaine at our office, but at that point no one was sure what was wrong. In all the confusion, I went to see Reg as soon as I could, truly believing that he had had a bit of a heart attack and they were going to operate to replace a valve. This was the night before the operation, and Reg is very nervous in hospitals at the best of times. Naturally he was in a bit of a state, so in my own way I tried to give him some confidence, explaining what would happen, that he should not worry and that he would be as fit as a fiddle and back to his beloved job before he knew it.

I was trying to tell him that the most painful thing about

having a heart valve operation is – so I have been told – the healing of the ribs afterwards. I told him that that would pass and he would soon be back on his feet. He looked really worried, and I told him, 'Come on, Reg, people have this operation all the time. It's routine, they're fantastic at it.'

'I didn't know they were going to do that and cut my chest open. I thought it was just my leg,' he said.

'Yes,' I blundered on, 'they do take something from your leg to put there.'

Silly sod; it's a good job I am only a doctor of letters and not one of medicine. Poor old Reg was now worse than when I went in. I wished him well and left for the evening. On my way out, I met Jill coming in. I told her what I had told Reg, reassured her that all would be well and said I would come back to see him the next day. But she answered, 'No, he's not having a heart valve. There is nothing wrong with his heart. He's just having the vein in his leg done. They're not touching his chest, Barry.' Oh dear, what had I done? In trying to make Reg feel better, I had made him feel a thousand times worse.

I left Jill to see Reg on her own, but as soon as I got home I phoned him up: 'Reg, whatever I have told you, take no notice. I don't know what I am talking about; they are not going to touch your heart.'

'I know, Sir [he always calls me Sir, no matter what I say to him]. You frightened the life out of me, but I know you only meant well.'

So you see, you can sometimes say too much or try to be too helpful.

Often unhelpful in life, and even more so in death, is bureaucracy. Take, for instance, Jack, who had recently lost his wife after only a short illness. A week after her cremation, he collected her ashes to be with him at home. A few days later, he received a letter from a bailiff for parking fines incurred on a car that his wife had sold some two years previously, fines that were obviously nothing to do with her. Jack naturally wrote back explaining this in some detail, but the reminders kept on arriving. When yet another £90 fine arrived in the post, all his letters obviously having been ignored, Jack had finally had enough, and he took the urn containing his wife's ashes and her death certificate to the Town Hall to place them under the nose of the manager of the parking department, who was naturally shocked. Do we really have to go to such lengths to be treated properly? Will Jack's actions be enough to stop the ridiculous continuation of unwarranted letters and fines? Or will he soon receive yet another letter, this time addressed to 'The Ashes of the Late Mrs Jones'? In this day and age, you never can tell.

I have, though, seen the agents of some bureaucracy come to the rescue. A recent East End funeral was for a local character, larger than life, with hundreds and hundreds of people attending. This fellow had walked a narrow line throughout his life and had spent a few years in prison to prove it. He had certainly never thought of the police as his best friends, but funny things often surround death, and respect steps in. The day before the funeral, the local florist had had so many orders that she had nowhere to put the flowers once she had made them up. Who should come to the rescue? Ironically, it was the police themselves. They opened up the old empty cells at the bottom of the police station where the flowers could be kept cold and safe, to be fresh for the funeral. He had not been able to avoid the long arm of the law this time! I could not resist including the story in the eulogy, which I had been asked to give, and the coincidence brought gales of laughter.

Some professionals could do with an encounter with the law themselves. My recently acquired Polish funeral director friend told me of a shocking incident he had come across in Poland. It was reported that ambulance men were being bribed by some funeral directors to tip them off about deaths. It was even suggested that some ambulance crews were so dependent on that money that they delayed the arrival of ambulances or, even worse, administered the wrong drugs, possibly hastening the patient's death. The horrible incident was brought to a conclusion when one particular ambulance man was sentenced after being accused of killing two patients in return for 30,000 zlotych (about £4,500) to inform a funeral home about patients' deaths. He had also falsified prescriptions for a muscle relaxant drug, which was believed to have killed at least two of his patients. It is a great honour to be recommended as a funeral director, but encouraging such unbelievable, immoral and corrupt behaviour to drum up trade is unacceptable.

In some countries, it is not as easy being a funeral director as it is here in the UK. Funeral directors from Zimbabwe, for example, have told me it is almost impossible to get fuel. Before a funeral director can buy fuel for his hearse, he must – unbelievably – display a corpse in an open coffin. Even then, he is given only just enough petrol to undertake the interment. In some areas it is worse, in that they have to take not only the deceased to the garage before they can buy any petrol, but also the bereaved family, along with documents proving that the deceased belongs to them. Absolutely incredible.

In countries such as Japan, there is a different kind of problem. The country boasts a huge cremation rate, but there is very little space for those who want to be buried, and a burial plot can cost as much as $86,000. At $28,000, even cryonics would be a much cheaper alternative. With either option, though, a serene eternity in the grave requires you to be something of a millionaire!

The most gruesome and perhaps one of the most difficult aspects of our work as funeral directors comes when we have to remove the dead. Here I do not mean just collecting somebody who has died from a hospital, a clinic or an old people's home in normal working hours. This in itself can be difficult enough, but what I really mean is what all the staff refer to as the 'night shift'. This out-of-hours service is covered by the staff on a rota covering nights and weekends. It is difficult work, often unsavoury. When that phone rings in the middle of the night, it wakes you with quite a jolt and you do not know what you are going to be asked to do next. Nobody enjoys this sort of work.

It is less of a problem when you are dealing with one of your local GPs or nursing homes, or perhaps a local family who have been nursing one of their kin at home. Then you know that everything is going to be clean and usually straightforward. However, the cases that present the funeral director with the most difficulty are what we call coroner's cases, cases that are referred to Her Majesty's coroner. These are usually sudden deaths or traumatic deaths, even murders or suicides. Sometimes they involve people who have died alone, often months before, but have only just been found. In all such cases, the funeral director's contribution is truly invaluable, and I respect and admire all my staff, and many others throughout the world, who undertake this part of their job so professionally.

Today, of course, the modern funeral director is well equipped with excellent ambulances, complete protective clothing, face masks, shoe covers, gloves, all-in-one cover suits, very efficient stretchers, trolleys and of course the inevitable body bags. You name it, they have it, so when we go out at night we are without doubt completely prepared. Despite that, it is certainly not a job for the squeamish. You need to work together in teams to get the best results, and the people who do this work have, I believe, always been underappreciated. When you arrive at the scene and you are faced with a messy situation, the team leader has to survey the situation and decide what has to be done. Make a quick plan. Be sure that the staff, the whole team, is of one mind. Prepare the equipment to be used. Then the most important part is to get in and out effectively, efficiently and as quickly as you can.

When I first started in the profession, however, we had very little equipment, just a fibreglass or, on some occasions, heavy wooden shell (a shell being a temporary coffin for the removal of the dead). If I am being honest, I can tell you that we did not have any protective clothing, gloves or other kind of hygiene equipment. We knew so little then, and we just got stuck in. The job had to be done, and we did not expect any other kind of help.

Deep inside, I think everybody must hold a fear of dying alone. An even greater fear might be to die alone and not be found for a long time. One such case I still remember today happened when I was around eighteen. It was a removal from the basement of a house just off the Old Kent Road. It was three in the morning when we arrived at the address. There were no lights because the electricity had been cut off, and we were working with just two torches provided by the police. The two policemen at the scene were looking very queasy when we arrived.

'Aw, mate,' one said, 'I couldn't do your job, not for a million pounds a week. We found this old fella, and I am sorry but I can't go in there again.'

With me was Micky Collins, a wonderful funny man who worked at Albin's for fifty years and was a kind of uncle to me. Luckily, Micky took charge. He had a lot of experience, and I trusted him completely. 'Get a torch, Barry, and follow me in,' he said.

As we walked down the stairs, the smell was indescribable. It was a little like burnt lard tinged with a putrefication gas, the effect of which was to make you heave. Holding hankies over our mouths, we entered the room. As the torchlight shone across the floor to the settee where the old gentleman was lying, I saw the body for the first time. I gasped in horror. 'Mick, he's moving, he's moving,' I cried.

'No he's not, Barry. Don't worry, boy, that's just the maggots and the lice.'

'Oh my God,' I thought. I had seen maggots before and had by now experienced a number of removals, but nothing quite like this. The whole body was moving with infestation. The doctor told the police that he would have been dead for several months in the height of summer. All these years later, I can still clearly see that old gentleman, smell that smell and even taste it, so deep in my consciousness it lies.

'Mick, this is terrible,' I said. 'What are we doing to do?'

'Well, boy, we are going to make a little plan here,' he replied. 'First of all, we'll get the torches set up so we've got a little bit of light shining on the body, and then we are going to bring the big shell down the stairs and put it right next to the settee. Now, because he will be stuck to the cushions, we'll take the cushions as well, so we're going to just slide him across into the shell, lid on, no messing around, straight up the stairs and out. Now you got it, boy?'

'All right, Mick, I won't let you down, I promise.'

'You're right,' he retorted, 'you won't, 'cos I can't be messed around, Barry boy. Just in and out, remember!'

So down the stairs we went with the big shell and positioned it right at the side of the settee. We went back upstairs to take a deep breath of air, tied our hankies around our mouths, went down again without hesitation and slid the gentleman, cushions and all, into the shell. Lid on, straight up on to our shoulders, up the stairs as quickly as possible, into the ambulance and off to the public mortuary. When we arrived at the old mortuary in Tennis Street, the mortician, who had already been alerted, was waiting. As we took the lid off the shell in clear light, the awful sight became fully visible and again the smell hit us. At this point, Mick and I had just about had enough. We were both heaving quite badly. Tom, the old mortician, said, 'Come on, you two posers, let's get on with it. The quicker it's away, the quicker we can go back to bed.' With one more gasp, we pulled the deceased from the shell, on to a tray and straight into the deep freeze. Mick and I washed the shell out with neat disinfectant, put it back on to the ambulance and went home.

I was staying at my nan's at the time, and when I arrived I got straight into the bath that she had all ready for me. As I removed my clothes, however, I noticed that there were maggots in my turn-ups and – don't ask me how – even a maggot in the back of my hair. Before I knew it, my nan had doused the bath – and me – with Lysol and put all my clothes, which I had left on the bathroom floor, into a plastic bag – some to be washed, some to be dry-cleaned, some to be thrown away. Half an hour later, I was red raw from the scrubbing and smelt like a sheep-dip, but I was as clean as a new pin. I did not sleep at all that night, what was left of it, and I definitely gave breakfast – and lunch – a miss the next day. All that I could taste or smell was that body. Luckily, I was soon back to normal. As for my nan, she was just the best. Throughout my whole life, I have had good people around me looking after me. That is really special, and very helpful when you are doing this kind of work.

Another case involved a deceased person who had been dead for some considerable time in reasonably hot weather. As we entered the flat in Pages Walk, Bermondsey, only a stone's throw from my old school, Bacon's, I noticed that there was lino on the floor rather than carpet. As you walked across the lino, you could hear this terrible crackling, crunching noise. I lifted a piece of lino back to find thousands of maggots that had crawled under the lino and had literally baked hard in the hot weather so that they crunched under your feet. But you will never guess what was underneath the maggots. The whole floor was covered with £5 notes, laid very carefully, Queen's head up. Yet this elderly lady, who had died in bed, led a very frugal lifestyle. Only a few sticks of furniture. Only lino on the floor. Nothing in the fridge or the cupboards. It was so unnecessary with all that money underneath the lino. The police were pretty impressed with my investigative skills, but if truth be known I was just being curious.

The smell in that flat was all the more sour because the dear old lady had actually dehydrated, having probably been there for months on end. It seems astounding that this could have occurred, but such events still happen. Surely somebody would have noticed that the rent was not being paid or the post was building up. Even the smell that would have come from the flat would have become atrocious at some stage.

On another awful occasion, a man died locked in a room with his Alsatian dog, only to suffer an awful fate after death. The room was in the basement of a huge empty house occupied only by this man. After days without food, the inevitable happened and the dog began to eat its owner. When we arrived, the sight was really horrific.

Also upsetting are the cases of suicide that I have attended.

Some where people have sealed up the cracks in doors, put the gas on in the oven and just lain down and gone to sleep. Some where people have shot themselves. Some where they have jumped from buildings. Others where they have hanged themselves. For one, I remember arriving at about four o'clock one morning to a body hanging from a tree in a churchyard in Kennington, unusual because the police normally cut the deceased down. It was an old tramp who, I guess, just could not face life any longer and, one cold winter's night, took his own life knowing that no one would miss him and perhaps no one would care. Well, I cared because I can still see him hanging there now. That particular case had a lasting effect on me and showed me the dreadful pain that loneliness must bring to some people.

There have also been accidents. I remember the shocking case of three men who had had a reasonable amount to drink and slept over at one of the number's homes. They had put the gas fire on in the living room, where they were lying on the floor on cushions. The gas meter was a slot meter (meaning you have to put money in it) and it ran out of money during the night, so of course the flame went out. The next morning the lady who lived in the house with her husband came down from the bedroom and went straight to the kitchen to put the kettle on. Noticing that the gas meter had run out of coins, she refilled it, not realising the catastrophe it would cause. In no time at all, the living room was full of gas and all three men were dead. I cannot imagine how that woman must have felt. Just a complete tragic accident. Yet another removal that I shall never forget.

I once visited an old people's home where a flu epidemic had taken hold. It was the third time we had been to the home that day, and the staff were in a real panic. As before, we reported to the front reception and went around to the back door, awaiting instructions. The poor nurse, who had been on duty for goodness knows how many hours working a double shift, was absolutely shattered. She met us at the back door and said, 'Come this way, Barry, it's just up on the first floor.'

Up we went. Each room was shared by three people, and when somebody dies but cannot be moved, the staff surround the bed with screens. The nurse showed us into the room and said, 'Mrs Jones is just behind the screens, Barry.' We moved the screens, put the shell on the floor and were about to take the lid off when this dear sweet little voice came from the bed, 'Not me, love, it's her over there; ain't my turn yet.' What a fright. They told me I went white as a sheet, as did the nurse standing behind me.

'Mrs Roberts, I am so sorry. What have I done?' the nurse cried.

'Don't worry, darling. It's a right laugh, innit, them thinking they got me and I'm still here. You've gotta laugh about it, girl. 'Ere, I don't mind going for a ride with ya, but not in that box.'

Although this was some twenty odd years ago, that dear lady, now in her nineties, is still as fit as a fiddle and I hope she goes on for ever. That's one removal I hope I never have to do. Thank goodness she saw the funny side of my trying to pre-empt her final departure.

Nowadays, it is rare that I go on removals, although I occasionally help out. For my sons and the staff, however, it is a regular occurrence, and despite the improvements in equipment, the tasks they face are every bit as bad. The removals undertaken today are just as sad, traumatic, sickening and, yes, even sometimes a little humorous, only underlining that we are the fourth emergency service and still everybody's last port of call! I expect there will always have to be a 'night shift' at Albin's. That's life – and death – for you. Definitely not for the squeamish.

6

COCKNEY FUNERALS

So what is a Cockney, you may well ask? Tradition suggests that, to be a true Cockney, you have to have been born within the sound of Bow Bells (which today, of course, never ring). But for me a true Cockney is a type of person living in a particular area on both sides of the River Thames – from Southwark Bridge and now expanding right up to the boundaries of Kent. I am quite proud to have been born a South London Cockney and absolutely love my roots. People think we talk funny in South London but we actually talk 'proper', probably more in the fashion of original English.

Cockney funerals have always been some of the proudest and most spectacular of funerals. In the early 1900s, a funeral would often cost as much as twenty times the average weekly wage. Today, the average funeral might cost perhaps five or six times the average weekly wage, so in real terms funerals are much cheaper than they were then. Cockney families were much more united in those days and often lived in the same house or the same street. Everybody would pull together.

When there was a death in the street, a local lady would be called upon to do the first washing. She would tie up the chin to stop the mouth setting open, put coins on the eyes simply to keep them closed by weight and cover the body in a white sheet. Her duties, 'the laying out' as this was called, were often done for kindness or for just a few pennies. All the mirrors in the house would then be covered up with white sheets, preventing any reflections of the past or the future. A white sheet placed over the window would immediately indicate to everybody that there had been a death in the house. Great respect was shown to this, and children would be prevented from playing outside the house.

The neighbours would then start what was called a subscription list. Around to every household they would go with a list provided by the undertaker. It simply said 'Subscription list on behalf of . . .', and there would go the name of the next of kin 'who requires assistance in the consequences of the loss of her late husband' or 'who requires assistance in the consequence of just a few flowers' depending on the widow or the widower's financial position. The list would then be numbered, often 1 to 80, and in would go the person, the name of the neighbour who made a contribution and the amount of money contributed. If somebody pledged tuppence, for example, but never came forward with the money, an X was put beside the name to show that he or she meant well but was finally, for some reason or other, not able to contribute. That list was then placed in the window of the deceased's home with a note of thanks from the family. If you had an X by your name, you were stigmatised, and that never went down well: you might even be shunned for quite some time. A popular person might have almost the whole cost of

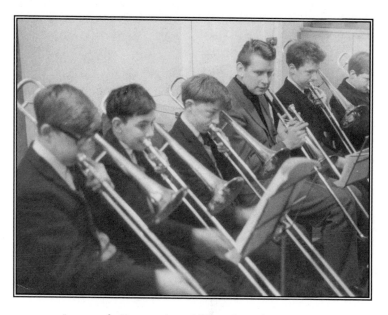

Images of a Bermondsey childhood: on the sofa with
nan, mum and dad and, below (foreground), learning the trombone.
That teacher with the teddy-boy haircut is Paul Carter, now
an organist who often plays at my funerals.

There's still little difference between the cockney funerals of today and days gone by. The top picture here dates from the early twentieth century and is one of those brought in by a family just when I was looking for such a photograph (see chapter 8).

It was common practice for the undertaker to supply
two 'mutes' for various duties during a funeral. Thanks to Brian
Parsons for this picture – there are many more fascinating images
from cockney funerals in his book, *The London Way of Death*.

These pictures illustrate part of the military ceremony involved in the repatriation of the body of a British soldier. They are always events of immense dignity and respect, with every move and step planned in advance in meticulous detail.

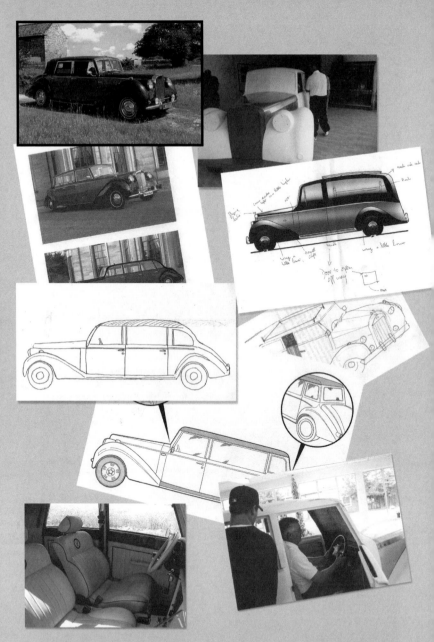

Just a few of the many notes, photos, designs and sketches I have built up
in the process of designing the Albin Royale, developed from the
original Royale model (inset).

When finished, the Albin Royale will become a proud member of our distinctive fleet (above), and a beautiful complement to our original Rolls-Royce (below).

Passion in all walks of life. That's me – squinting – in the front row left of the Bacons School team line-up (thanks to Keith Kennard for the photo). The whole forward line played for Bermondsey and South London, including me! And, below, as International Undertaker of Mystery, Austin Powers. I know which performance I'm most proud of!

the funeral raised on a subscription list, making life very easy for the family. This togetherness, this 'we was all one' kind of thinking, gave great comfort and security. For me, this example depicts what a Cockney really is.

In Bermondsey, where I grew up, once all the old cemeteries had disappeared and the churchyards had been filled, there was no cemetery space whatsoever. The only cemeteries they could use were private cemeteries such as Nunhead, Manor Park, East London and St Patrick's, Leytonstone, one of the only Catholic cemeteries available to the Catholic community that is still used today. Over the past hundred years, a great number of families have been buried some distance from Bermondsey itself, so it is not unusual that, even today, we still cross the water and travel to cemeteries like Leytonstone. One of our great traditions is never to take anyone through the Rotherhithe Tunnel. If we are going across a river, we use a bridge. The Cockney saying 'Never take anybody underground before their time' is something I still strictly adhere to today, no matter what the traffic is like.

When a Cockney Catholic funeral used to arrive at St Patrick's, Leytonstone, the single death bell would chime as you went through the gate, as it still does today. Unimaginable as it seems to us now, it was not uncommon for one priest to undertake a service in the small chapel for two or even three families at once. Many of the graves were over by what we called 'the railway', a piece of ground situated right alongside the railway weaving in and out of London. This was an extremely long walk for the funeral director, particularly with a heavy coffin and many flowers, so while the family were having the service in the little church, the cars would pull round as near as they could to the grave and remove all the flowers.

As the deceased was then carried directly from the church and past the flowers that had been laid out, the family would, by tradition, each pick up a wreath and follow the deceased to the graveside, a practice that still often happens today. I saw this recently at a family funeral for Joanna Downes, who works with me and often helps me so much with my writing. She has a wonderful old-fashioned Catholic Cockney family and the funeral was at Leytonstone. Her Aunty Eileen, a Cockney character larger than life, said to some of the younger members of the family, 'Come on, now, help the undertakers, pick up a wreath each like we did years ago. It's a big honour and a tradition.' These people are the salt of the earth; to them tradition is everything.

You can be a Cockney no matter which side of the river you live on, but the divide of the Thames between East London and South London can sometimes seem like an ocean. Anybody living in South London who has been out late at night across the river will know just how hard it is to get a cabbie to come to the south side, unless of course he lives in South London or Kent himself. Of course, the people of London have always lived in tribes, and in a small way still do. It seems too that the Thames was once also a place where Londoners disposed of their dead. The Museum of London displays over five hundred objects and human remains retrieved from the river by archaeologists. So many skulls have come out of the Thames that it is felt to be inevitable that it was once a burial ground. Maybe a thousand years ago they would just have weighted the bodies down and thrown them in. London's history, particularly this aspect, never ceases to amaze me.

The *Daily Mail* newspaper has run a piece called 'Every Picture Tells a Story', in which a person or family can send in an old picture with a story or some link to the past. One picture, published in late 2003 and showing some Cockneys in South London in 1923, featured an ancestor of the person who had submitted the photograph. It told this sad but interesting story:

This photo of my father and his friends was taken outside a pub in West Lane Bermondsey South London in 1923 when I was four years old, I am now eighty-four. It was during the depression and work was very scarce but my father, also called Bill, had heard that there was work going in East India Docks on the other side of the Thames. He went to the entrance of the Rotherhithe Tunnel to get a lift to the Docks but slipped under the wheels of a lorry and was killed. He was buried in Nunhead Cemetery by the firm Albin & Sons which has been featured in the ITV series *Don't Drop the Coffin*.

That last little bit made me feel very proud. You see, we are the custodians of the memories of the past. Our ledgers hold the key to the community, family histories and the way, of course, we honour our dead. They are a sacred treasure.

Mr Knox, a local funeral director whose business we purchased in the early 1970s, was a good friend of the Albin family. He was a man of very strict morals and principles. The Co-op, as it is called in South London, originated as a grocer's and offered a good deal to all people purchasing their foods, as well as a dividend, the famous Co-op 'Divi'. When the Co-op entered the world of funeral directing, some time in the mid-1900s, I believe, Mr Knox forbade his family to purchase any groceries from the Co-op store as a protest about their entering the sacred area of the funeral market. Today, of course, the Co-op is an accepted funeral director, probably one of the biggest funeral directors in the UK. At Albin's, we try to get along with all funeral directors. Our philosophy is always to be able to offer or receive a helping hand.

The fascinating piece below, called *Cockney Funerals*, is a transcript of a recording made for BBC radio in the late 1950s/early 1960s. Arranged by C.A. Ladbrooke and produced by David Thompson, it is truly 'Albin's'.

The reminiscences of two brothers, Mr Arthur and Mr Ernest Albin, whose family have been undertakers for several generations in Bermondsey.

Mr Arthur Albin, the elder brother, now in his late sixties, speaks first:

My grandfather and my father were undertakers for over the last hundred years and always in the same locality, South East London. My father took over from me grandfather and started in a place at the side of Guy's Hospital. He eventually married; he married a nurse and brought her to the shop, transformed her from a nurse into an undertaker's wife. She filled the position admirably, and when Father was out conducting funerals, Mother were quite capable of booking orders in his absence. I was born within the precincts practically of Guy's Hospital. I attended Bacon's School in Grange Road and when I left there I were going to follow in the same footsteps as me father as an undertaker. After a few years the First World War came; I had to go. When I was de-mobbed I came out and from there on I started with me father again.

In those days horses were 100 per cent used – there was no such thing as a motor car, not for a funeral. A fair animal would cost 60 guineas but my father would say, 'Well, why pay 60 guineas when I can go over to Holland and,' he said, 'I can buy perhaps three for a hundred guineas,' and he used to go over to Holland every second year; he used to go over on a ship called the Ben Bow from Tower Bridge. On the third or fourth occasion he said to me, 'Would you like to come to Holland?' I said yes I would so he said, 'All right, I'll take you with me.' We went to Holland, we went to Flushing, and we got off the boat and went up country a little way. I can't quite tell you the name of the farm or the district but these funeral horses were bred in Holland just as the English Shire horse is bred in England, and he used to take us out on the farm see if there was anything we liked; see, the idea was they was to be 100 per cent black, black horses for funerals, and the only way you could guarantee for a horse to be black all the year round was a stallion for that is an entire horse. Once a horse became a gelding, once they broke their coat, they always took on a brownish looking coat and we have had people pass remarks at times, they said, 'That's a brown horse, not a black one,' and of course stallions were very, very hard to handle. The great thing was that when you had them on the pole you mustn't let their heads get too close; if you were stationary, always have a side rein so that they couldn't take any chances with them getting to one another, you know, then you were all right with them. If you once let them go and they started to sort of fight it was very dangerous.

The earliest that I can remember they used to walk to the cemeteries, and the method that they used to use in those days was that the undertaker used to supply bearers to start with. They used to walk away from the house with the coffin on their shoulders with a pair of trestles strapped on top and they used to start walking. Well, after about twenty minutes they used to get tired and when it came to a change over to a fresh set of men, which normally used to be supplied by the family, they used to stop at the nearest public house en route, the trestles were then taken away from the top of the coffin, the coffin was then put on the trestles and everybody would adjourn inside the public house for ten minutes to quarter of an hour for refreshments, and after they had that they would come out, the fresh set of men would take up the coffin, the trestles would be placed back on top and this used to happen en route all the way to the cemetery, and it could possibly take them four hours to walk to a cemetery so you can imagine by the time they got to the cemeteries the state that everybody was in.

Prior to the funeral taking place, when the body was eventually placed in its coffin in its home, the undertaker had to supply what was known as two mutes. Now these two mutes were dressed as undertakers normally are, in black, and they had to carry what was known as a wand, a wooden pole with a brass top, and attached was a bow or material. Now depending on the person dead, the material was used. If you were a very wealthy costermonger and owned three/four barrows he would have what was known as a silk funeral; those bows were then made of silk, and around the men's silk hats was also a band tied round into a big bow, which laid down the back of the hat and down the man's back; that was also made of silk. If on the other hand he was a normal costermonger, perhaps with one barrow, he would have a cotton funeral.

We used to have to send those two mutes round to the house or the shop, wherever the funeral was taking place, and they stood each side of the door and they were sort of porters: as mourners came they opened the door for them. I think they were called mutes because their duty was to stand perfectly still and open the door when requested. They were like two statues. We had a very big funeral once of a publican and we send the mutes round at twelve o'clock, two hours prior to us going to the funeral. Well, if they'd just done their duties as they should have done they would have been there when we got there to do the funeral; the people, the mourners, kept coming and bringing them inside to have a drink, so that when we got there they could hardly stand they'd had so many drinks waiting. Not their fault, but people kept enticing them to bring the men in to have a drink; well, they had so many when we got there they were absolutely useless, it was a matter of whether they could stand.

First of all, what precedes the hearse is a man carrying what we term a lid of feathers. Now a lid of feathers is a board made in the shape of a coffin lid which had six iron brackets fixed on the top and each of those iron brackets were fixed into plumes, all ostrich feathers done on copper wire; of course, you would say to me how could he carry it with a silk hat on, but he had to discard the silk hat and he had a pad on his head exactly the same as when the men on a Sunday afternoon of the same decade used to come round with muffins and crumpets and ring a bell. Now this fella carrying the board of feathers had that on his head and he held the side of the board. Mind you, on a day with no wind they were very easy to carry but they were very hard to carry if there was any wind. He preceded the hearse. Now we could run six horses on the hearse but police regulations did not permit six horses to be driven by one man, you had to have a postillion, that was a man riding on the near-side front leader; now that's what we called a set, and that was the real thing for a big funeral, six horses. There were feathers on the horses' heads except the one postillion, because if you had a feather on that horse you would have obscured his view, you see, so you eliminated that feather, but carrying on with some more feathers right on top of the hearse was a set of hearse feathers.

It was an old custom come down from the ages and I am afraid its origin has been lost in antiquity – we can only presume that it was something to scare off evil spirits, any evil spirit who might have designs on the soul of the person who was lying inside that hearse. They took over the job of keeping the evil spirits away, apart from the undertaker's men who would walk at the side of the coffin with a baton which was of wood with either silver ends or brass ends which were very highly decorative, and officially their job was also to keep evil spirits from attacking the body from the side ways. Now you would possibly ask me what was the idea of undertaker's assistants walking by the side of the hearse with truncheons. Now the idea of a truncheon would go back many, many years. You have no doubt heard of the expression of body-snatchers; well, that was going back so many years when the college of anatomy wanted a body and they'd been known to steal a body, and it's been told to us that the men were given those truncheons to ward off any idea of anybody taking the body.

With regards to the coster funeral of many years ago, that was in the time when unions first started and he was quite a high official in this union and the funeral went from Bermondsey to Leytonstone. We walked the entire journey, which is approximately ten miles. The hearse was drawn by six horses. The horses all had plumes on their heads and the hearse was covered with ten plumes which stood approximately four foot six high. They were all made of black ostrich plumes and this particular funeral was with the six horses and the hearse and ten coaches following behind all drawn by four horses, and leading the entire cortège were the old banners that the unions and the old associations used to have. I should think they measured at least sixteen foot across and approximately ten foot deep. I should say there were about eight of these banners. There must have been about two hundred men in the procession, and that funeral went from Bermondsey, it started off about nine o'clock, they eventually arrived at St Patrick's Cemetery Leytonstone about one o'clock in the afternoon. The service and the burial in the cemetery took about an hour to hour and a half and then they all arrived back home in Bermondsey about ten o'clock that night, because after they left the cemetery they all adjourned to a public house immediately outside the cemetery – they stayed there for about two hours. From there they came on to another well-renowned stopping place for funerals in those days in Leytonstone, The Thatched House, and I had personally seen outside The Thatched House forty coaches of funerals, not all the same funeral, but of funerals all adjourned where the people had gone into The Thatched House for refreshment. After they would leave The Thatched House, they would come down the Mile End Road and their final stop was a public house just near the Minories before they came back over Tower Bridge before they arrived home.

Sometimes the greatest occasion in a man's life was his funeral. Today it would be impossible. You see, a successful costermonger really wanted for us to make the most show of a funeral and the most show we could; they'd think that they are paying the deceased as much respect as they possibly can so that his memory or that funeral lasts in people's minds for years and years, and really it added to the costermongers' tradition. If they give their relatives a funeral like that they were always something to look up to. It was something to look up to because the days that I am speaking of was before cremation when the deceased remains was more sacred than what it is today. Now today the human body is practically nothing. Seventy per cent now of people are cremated. Now it seems to have lost that sort of respect for the human body, the body that you have known, the face that you have known. Now in the days thirty to forty year ago the memory of a mother or a father lying in a coffin that we would have embalmed, so that when their memory focused back to their mum or dad, they could see them lying in their coffin restful, just as if they looked at them lying in bed, but I am afraid that today that tradition is past, it's past. People years ago would not only have a body buried, but rather than it should be in contact with the ground they would have a brick grave dug, and many a costermonger today lays in a brick-lined grave so that he is in no contact with the earth at all, and that coffin is on iron bearers, the body is in a leaden coffin in another oak case, and the body was embalmed, and if that coffin was opened today after thirty or forty years that body should be in a good state of preservation. But the body today is not remembered as such. It is nothing; today you put it in a furnace – in an hour you're reduced to ashes and that's it. It's gradually coming that funerals in the sense of the word will go; a person will die, they will be taken away, they're cremated, two or three weeks after there will be a memorial service held at a local church that will be the actual funeral, not the disposal of the body.

* * *

Arthur and Ernest Albin had an enormous influence on my early life, along of course with Fred Albin and my dad George. Between them, I guess they modelled my early days. Ernie was very well-spoken and smoked large King Edward cigars. We were living over the shop, and Ernie would send up a piece of *The Times* newspaper, which he had every day, and get me to read a small piece out to him. When I was quite young, probably around eight, I was knocked over in Spa Road by a post office van, which ultimately came off worse, I have to tell you. When I was taken home after being in hospital, Ernie would pop up occasionally during the day and took the time to teach me to play chess, a game that even today I occasionally enjoy.

When I was young, Ernie was not seen out on funerals very much. The really big influence on funerals was Arthur, a wonderful tall stout man with an incredible presence. A genuine, proud and elegant man, he was so kind to me and my parents, and always treated us as an extension of his family. He would often write and remind us of that after he had retired! Once a week he would come down from his retirement in Brighton by train to London Bridge, where his son Fred or my dad would pick him up; and he would spend the whole day at the shop talking to everybody, standing in the window chatting to his old friends. Arthur would always take a little time to speak with me, giving me lots of words of encouragement and wisdom. I am so lucky and grateful to have known him. He had no airs and graces, only lots of humour and strength.

What does not come across from the transcription of great reminiscences of those two brothers Arthur and Ernest Albin is a difference in their accents and in the tone of humour in their voices, yet we can still decipher their care and pride in the profession into which they were born. I have listened to the tape of the programme hundreds, perhaps thousands, of times, but I never get bored with it or fail to find something new in it. Importantly, Arthur was even then, in the late 1970s/early 1980s, lamenting what he described as the end of a funeral as we know it. He had not been that fond of the transition from horses to motor hearses, but he truly felt that cremation would sound the end of the funeral. You would just be picked up, carted off, cremated and that would be the end of it, maybe a few people getting together, as he says, for a memorial service. For a short time it looked as if he could be right, but then, in the late 1960s/early 1970s, I noticed a complete turn in people's approach towards funerals. Tradition, honour and perhaps most importantly sacredness began to reappear in the structure of a funeral, an approach that has grown and grown. How pleased and proud Ernie and Arthur would be to see the Cockney funeral alive and well, so to speak, in Bermondsey.

There were other formative people in my life too. My mum, of course, being the only woman living at the shop, looked after everybody, but what I could never lose and what she gave me in abundance was love. She was admired and cared for by everybody who knew her. Fred and my dad, George, helped to model my business life and my character and gave me one of the greatest gifts of all – security. Both are still alive and well with me today. How lucky I have been, and how lucky I still am. I cannot imagine a day in my life without them there. Fred was the greatest boss I could have had and Dad by far the greatest father. Yet again I digress and am lost in the sentimentality of the people who have so wonderfully touched my life.

Bermondsey has always been quite a cosmopolitan area in its own way. A number of wonderful Italian families have settled here. Several Jewish families owned and worked in many local businesses and shops. Add to that a wonderful Irish community, and today Bermondsey is also embracing and adapting to a number of new cultures which have brought with them their own funeral rites. Unlike Mr Arthur, I do not ever envisage the end of the funeral as we know it. All over the world, I have witnessed funerals that are meaningful, caring and engulfed in ritual and strong tradition, but you will never see anything like a Cockney funeral.

Some forty years ago, television broadcast a programme called *Down Any Street*, which was never repeated. I still remember sitting watching it – in black and white, of course. The programme was to follow a local Bermondsey family, the Snows, through a new birth, a twenty-first birthday party and a christening. What the makers of the programme had not anticipated, however, was that the family would suffer a death and, perhaps for the first time ever, allow the cameras to share the grief and reality of the funeral service with them. Who should be the family funeral director? You got it – Albin's, in the good old Bermondsey tradition!

As there were no videotapes in those days, we all thought that the show had been lost in antiquity, but one of the younger members of the Snow family, Bobby, a real local Bermondsey boy who runs his own business up on Crystal Bridge, was determined to recover the original film. After about seven years of endless letters and phone calls to the independent television companies, Granada (who had made the programme) being one of them, Bobby eventually discovered the film in its original format. Not without some expense, he was able to recover it from its own burial place

111

deep in an old warehouse along with thousands of other films. Bobby, always one of the most generous of people, made sure of course that I was one of the first to get a copy.

The programme is about an hour and a half long, the first twenty minutes being completely devoted to the funeral itself. Filming was based around the Millpond Estate in Bermondsey and Rotherhithe.

As well as the Snow family, the programme featured my dad, Fred, Micky Collins, Ron, Keith, Teddy, Lewis, all the old staff I remember as a boy, as well as the wonderful Mr Brodie, superintendent of the St Patrick's Leytonstone cemetery. It is a really wonderful film that everybody should watch. I am sure television companies should show old films like these again – viewers would love them.

This was a good old-fashioned Cockney funeral, with the deceased lying at home in the front room. We see the widow saying her final goodbyes to her husband. We even see the body itself lying in the coffin. We witness the final fastening of the coffin and the ceremonial carrying from the house, the seating of the family in the cars and the traditional walking away from the house – paging, as we call it – the arrival at the cemetery, some of the funeral service, at the graveside and the funeral tea afterwards, where all were welcome in true Cockney fashion. The last part of the programme is the truly beautiful christening, with lovely old Father McKenna from Paradise Street welcoming the child into the church.

As I watched, I have to confess that I shed a tear for my past too. Looking at all those men, then young, who have been such an influence on my life, and realising that so few of them are with us today, left me a bit melancholy. To see Dad, Fred and Micky Collins looking so young, strong, full of hope and anticipation, swift of foot, dark-haired and quite handsome really, was a bit like stopping time for a moment. It was so moving that I have not been able to watch it again since, but the film has of course now joined Albin's archives, and when the time is right I know I will watch it again. It and the wonderful Cockney tape reproduced above will help to preserve these people and our memories for ever.

As for the future, it is safe with me, my sons and the wonderful Albin's staff who dedicate their daily life to the people they serve. Others may try to introduce changes – just today, I received an e-mail from Detroit, USA, announcing that the 'Cryonics Institute has its fifty-first human whole-body patient, a Californian cancer victim. Washout and perfusion were done at the California Mortuary.' But despite all these new ideas and unusual practices, there will always be Cockney funerals in South London, don't worry about that. So, just like the title of the book, you can 'bury my heart (and preferably the rest of me, please) in Bermondsey' – but definitely not in Detroit, thanks very much.

7

ALWAYS A HORIZONTAL
PASSENGER

The Soldier

If I should die, think only this of me:
That there's some corner of a foreign field
That is for ever England. There shall be
In that rich earth a richer dust concealed;
A dust whom England bore, shaped, made aware,
Gave, once, her flowers to love, her ways to roam
A body of England's, breathing English air,
Washed by the rivers, blest by the suns of home.

And think, this heart, all evil shed away,
A pulse in the eternal mind, no less
Gives somewhere back the thoughts by England given;
Her sights and sounds; dreams happy as her day;
And laughter, learnt of friends; and gentleness,
In hearts at peace, under an English heaven.

Rupert Brooke (1887–1915)

What this wonderful poem, written when Rupert Brooke was a private in the First World War, shows me is his fear of dying abroad and not returning to his beloved England, a fear shared by so many of us, even today. There is something very special about returning to your homeland, your roots, and wanting to end your life where you began it. For me, especially, being buried in England, specifically in Bermondsey, is very important (of course, I want to be dead first), but be assured, wherever I die in the world, coming back to England is a priority and a wish that has been made very clear in my last instructions.

International repatriation has always been the part of the work of the funeral director that I have enjoyed and admired the most. As a young man at Albin's, it was always fascinating to be called, as we often were, to Nuffield House, the private part of Guy's Hospital, to arrange a repatriation of somebody from another part of the world who had perhaps come here for medical treatment but had died. Over the years, I think I have repatriated people who have died here to almost every corner of the world. It is a complex business with many international rules to abide by, and each country of course has its own tradition or method of abiding by these rules.

Generally speaking, though, five specific documents are required: a copy of the Death Certificate from the official entry of death; a coroner's Out of England Certificate, giving permission for the deceased to leave the country; an Embalming Certificate, given by the embalmer and stating that the deceased has been scientifically and hygienically embalmed to an international standard; a doctor's or pathologist's Free From Infection Certificate, stating that the deceased has no contagious disease that could be taken from the UK to the country of destination; and finally the Funeral Director's Declaration that the deceased has been sealed hermetically (airtight) into a metal-lined coffin, and that the deceased, and only the deceased, has been placed in that coffin, and therefore the deceased is in a safe and sanitary condition for the journey.

Those of you who read my last book, *Final Departures*, will recall my work on the International Pass for the Dead, a document I designed that, in number order, in twenty or so languages, enables you almost to self-translate the documentation and information concerning the deceased. These standard five documents, having usually been certified by the embassy of the country concerned, are then placed in the International Pass file for the dead. These travel with the deceased, enabling the deceased with the coffin to pass through customs wherever necessary. The coffin usually receives a diplomatic stamp preventing anybody from opening it until its final destination, as well as clearance from the government concerned.

All methods of transportation – sea, rail, road – are used for repatriation, but by the most common form of long-distance transport for the deceased today is of course air, and I am sure you will be absolutely astonished to hear how often this happens. Many of the aircraft we travel on to our holiday destinations and business venues are carrying a deceased person to what will often be their final destination.

Through my work with Airline Mortuary Services in America (AMS), I was to have an interesting insight into how these special passengers are referred to in the airline business. When they are placed on the flight load computer, they are referred to as 'HRs' or 'HUMs', short of course for 'Human Remains'. The cargo agents are very careful never to place HRs on the same flight as dogs (animals being known as

'AVIs'). It is a known fact in the industry that dogs are completely spooked by human remains and become very unsettled. People do say, don't they, that dogs and cats have extrasensory perception. Whatever it is, HRs and dogs are never loaded together. I have personally had human remains removed from a flight that had a number of dogs travelling on it that were already booked and loaded and could not be removed or changed.

Although the official name for the travelling dead is Human Remains, HRs or HUMs, the staff who work in the industry, particularly those working in the AMS, refer to them as 'horizontal passengers'. The handlers in America, the people who have to lift the coffins and the deceased into the cargo hold of the plane, tend to refer to them as 'dead weights' or, more affectionately, 'silent cargo'. For many of them, I think, it is just the way of dealing with something that they find extremely frightening, perhaps the part of the job they least understand or enjoy.

For me, I cannot and will not change the habits of a lifetime; I refer to each HR by his or her first names and surname because for me it is all so very real, and although of course we have to use abbreviations and numbers on documentation and computers, we should never forget that these are very real people who have lived very real lives and we are the custodians of their final journey. Many AMS clients have been 'snow-birds', people who have migrated for the winter from New York to Maine. Upon death, AMS flies them back to New York for burial.

When travelling on airlines, human remains usually travel at double the cargo rate. Some airlines offer a flat-rate deal (no pun intended), but in most situations the final cargo fee is assessed according to weight or a maximum size, whichever is the greater. When repatriation was completed by rail (which eventually priced itself out of the market), a whole carriage on its own would be used for a human remains so you would have to pay for the whole carriage, which became impractical.

The first repatriation I ever remember going on was by road. I was a young lad and my dad was picking somebody up from Wales and taking them back by road. He said I could join him for the experience. I remember that the weather was really bad, and the roads were a lot slower then, as were the vehicles. We travelled in our little Bedford van. I recall the weather being so bad that Dad had to fit chains on the tyres. The van had a bier in the centre of it that almost divided the van in half from top to bottom. This was of course so that you could get more than one coffin in the van at a time, one on top, one underneath. I cannot remember how long the journey to Wales was, but it seemed like for ever. Mum had packed sandwiches, a nice hot flask and our favourite biscuits. We had some cushions, blankets and a little paraffin heater for emergencies.

We collected the deceased and began our journey back. By now, Dad was pretty tired so he pulled off the road into a small lay-by and made us both a snug little bed in the back under the bier. It was a real adventure for me, and I loved every minute of it. I don't remember it being cold in the back of that van, and I didn't give a second thought to there being somebody dead above us. I was with my dad, I was never afraid when I was with him, and we had hot tea, lovely biscuits and sandwiches.

I had my goodies and went straight off to sleep. Next thing I remember was the sound of cows rushing past the van and mooing (as they do) on their way to being milked. Dad told me to stay where I was to try and get a bit more sleep while he began the journey home. It was so cosy, and I am sure the gentleman we collected did not mind sharing with us, just as we did not mind sharing with him (he had the top bunk, after all). When we arrived home, Dad dropped off me and the deceased at Tranton Road, where our chapel and our home were at the time. Although it was very late, Dad went straight round to the garage and washed the van off ready for the next day.

We had had a fabulous day, and he was – and still is – a fabulous dad and a great benchmark for me. So you see, I guess collecting somebody from Wales was my first repatriation job, and I have been on many such journeys since all over the UK and some of Europe, on occasions being accompanied by my own sons, history repeating itself. Thank God that the vehicles are better and faster these days, even though the work is the same.

Albin's has, during its lifetime, had quite a wide experience overall with repatriation, being situated where we are with all the docks around us. There were Norwegian, Finnish and Swedish churches surrounding us and of course Nuffield House, where now and in the old days wealthy people were treated, many from other countries. Much of our repatriation work came from there and from the sailors who visited our docks and ports. Today, we still have a wonderful relationship with our Scandinavian churches, Nuffield House and the much newer London Bridge Hospital. The very professional and caring staff at this well-run and well-supervised private hospital call me whenever they have a death as they do not have a mortuary; they quite correctly use mine at Culling Road. After all, if we pay for our treatment, we subconsciously do not really expect to die, so it is not surprising that there are no mortuary facilities. There is, I'm glad to say, rarely a death, but we remove the deceased when there is.

As I have already mentioned, I have always found repatriation to be one of the most intriguing parts of our business, and I am sure that it was this fascination that led me to look at different funeral practices all over the world. Whenever I hear we have a repatriation to a country that we have not dealt with before, I insist on knowing all about it. Even today, the mystery of this area still holds great interest for me, and I expect it always will.

I have often looked at the people whom we repatriate and wondered what their life held for them; even at school, I used to love looking at the pictures of people in Africa in our geography books. What was it like growing up in the country where they were born? What had they seen in life? How did they end up dying here in London? What would it mean to their family when they arrived home? How important it was, when that sealed coffin was opened or the family looked through the coffin's purpose-built face glass, for the family to see that person they had loved so much. How important it was for that moment to be perfect – and it was my responsibility to make it perfect. In life, that person and I would often, because of language difficulties, have been unable to communicate with words; but in death words could cause no confusion, all was clear, and that person's remains were, as in all cases, sacred.

Interestingly, many of the big liners that take people on wonderful long cruises around the world have mortuary refrigeration installed so that the cruise can continue uninterrupted when a death occurs, and the deceased can be returned to their desired destination when the ship docks. Repatriation is so fascinating that many books and films have touched on the subject. One such film, called *Avanti!*, which stars Juliet

Mills and Jack Lemmon, looks with great humour and kindness on not just a great love story, but also inadvertently – with a little farce – the difficulties that can occur with repatriation, particularly when it is not really wanted. Let me explain.

The film is set around a beautiful hotel on the coast of Italy where two deaths have occurred. One is of a famous American senator, the other of a lovely quaint English lady. The son of the senator, played by Jack Lemmon, and the daughter of the English lady, played by Juliet Mills, fly to the hotel to arrange the repatriation and interment of their parents, where they meet for the first time. They eventually discover that, for two weeks every year for the past twenty years, his father and her mother have met at the hotel, where they have had a secret affair. Although being deeply in love, they would then leave and not meet or speak again until the next year. The American senator is to be flown back to America with full military honours, while the English lady is to be buried by the sea where she died in Italy, a place they both loved so much.

Now, Italy is the most highly regulated country for repatriation. You need documents for everything. Stamps from mayors and local councillors, payments for each separate document. We are given a really funny insight into the son's preparations when the mayor turns up and, opening his coat and briefcase, lays out about twenty different documents on the lid of the coffin . . . and then five different kinds of stamp. Each document has to be stamped three times – boom, boom, boom – with a fee, of course, for each 'boom'. Very true and very funny. In the midst of all this, of course, these two people fall in love themselves. History ends up repeating itself as they continue the affair that their father and mother had had, meeting every year for two weeks.

The final twist in the tale comes right at the end, when a

waiter who has worked all his life in the hotel, but has always wanted to be an American and live in America, suddenly dies. Seizing the opportunity, they switch the bodies, and the waiter is sent to America to be given a state funeral, something he would have loved, while the senator is buried quietly and lovingly alongside his English lady. What a charming and beautiful end. If you ever get the chance to see it, this is a great film and well worth watching.

But back to reality! In my early days of repatriation, shipping people all over the world, I would regularly receive calls from the Iranian Embassy asking me to go to the Harley Street Clinic and collect someone who had died there, also meeting the family and making all the arrangements to send them and the deceased back to Iran. I often turned up at the same time as Chris Henley, one of the repatriation staff with the funeral directors Kenyon's. He would have been called, perhaps by the director of the clinic, to assist the family, so there we would both be in reception, waiting to see the same family to do the same job. There were lines drawn and rules of honour, and, both being honourable people, we would step back from an area that was not ours. If, for example, the family were Iranian, this was considered to be my area because of the embassy. If they were Egyptian, this would be Christopher's because Kenyon's looked after the Egyptian Embassy. There were never any real arguments, just a little light banter, and we established a friendship that still exists today.

Kenyon's have always, I feel, been the leaders in repatriation in the UK. Kenyon Air Transportation Ltd (KAT) was the first, and is still the only, funeral directors to date to be part of IATA (the governing body of the airline industry) – quite a feat, I have to tell you. Having always remained friends with Christopher, it was a great achievement and honour when we were able to purchase KAT, which we now call KCH (Kenyon Christopher Henley Ltd) in a three-way partnership with myself as Chairman, Christopher as Chief Executive and my dear friend Peter Hindley, the head of Dignity Funerals and the previous sole owner of the company, as a Director. This union has been overwhelmingly successful, and you would not believe some of the amazing repatriations we take part in.

One such case involved the late great Donald Pleasance, famous film, television and stage actor, who died in his home in the south of France and was brought back by myself to London, where we undertook his cremation. I have told the story of this in some detail in a previous book, but it is worth repeating that this was a great honour and privilege, although most of all a big responsibility with the media watching everything in detail. No room for error in flight delays. No margin for the misbooking of dogs (remember the start of the chapter?) – one or the other would have to be put on another plane. No, it had to be exactly right, and it was.

Christopher took responsibility a few years ago for the repatriation of a famous Indian Chief called Long Wolf who had been buried here as long ago as 1892. The exhumation was completed early, as always, one spring morning with Christopher supervising the whole event. There were many elders from the Chief's tribe in North America, and Christopher escorted the body with the elders privately back to the happy hunting land and burial grounds of this Indian tribe at Wounded Knee. (This too was where I got my idea for the title of this book – bury my heart in Bermondsey, though, not in Wounded Knee.) Christopher underwent with the tribe the ceremony of the burial of the dead, something he has never forgotten and is extremely proud of.

I think that moment probably changed his life a bit. This often happens when you are dealing with different cultures and the sacredness of such an event. For the head mourners, it was a kind of completion of a circle and a wonderful event in their history. We tend to approach everything in this life by looking at the labels that immediately identify the people we deal with. Christopher is one of those rare people who see past the label to what is underneath.

Going to a particular country to effect a repatriation directly is becoming more common these days. Applying all our know-how, skills and equipment, a team recently flew to the Falkland Islands to recover the remains of a scientist who had been working there in extraordinarily low temperatures reaching into the thirties below. While doing her work, she had dressed in a seal-like thermal wet suit because she had briefly to enter the water, where she was possibly mistaken for a penguin and killed by an animal that attacks them. There had to be a pathologist's report and a full enquiry, of course, but no embalming or repatriation could be completed while the body was at such a low temperature, indeed frozen solid. It took months to be able to undertake the investigation and the duties of the repatriation. To be honest, you could never imagine a funeral director or embalmer being involved in such a case, or that such a situation could happen, but believe me that is true. At Albins and KCH, you never know what you are going to face next.

One of the most difficult and most moving parts of our recent work has been the repatriation of soldiers and war civilians who have died abroad. The respectful and moving ceremony that surrounds their return is something I regard with great seriousness and as a great honour. Christopher has professionally led our staff, including my son Simon, in this work on a number of war zone visits to Basra, Baghdad and Afghanistan. We respect that so much related to this work has to remain totally confidential, but I can clearly state some things of great importance to the good people who undertake these responsibilities. First and foremost, the professionalism, attention to detail, sensitivity and commitment with which this work is completed by the military departments involved is outstanding and should be truly commended.

I also admire Christopher's ability and the obvious esteem in which he is held by the military. He has worked for a number of years now in preparing these contracts and advising and supporting the various departments. More recently, my staff and myself have been able to help him in this difficult work. What I also admire about Christopher is his willingness to be first to stand up, ready to lead a team to any part of the world at a minute's notice and never putting his staff where he is not willing to be himself. In fact, if Christopher could concentrate on one thing at a time, he would be the perfect human being (but that would be impossible for Chris – he's far too active and is always working too hard!).

I have always maintained that, as funeral directors, we cannot afford to be judgmental. We have to complete the tasks that are presented to us effectively, efficiently and often without question. So whatever our feelings are concerning war or the political decisions that are made to take us to war, this must come second to our responsibility, just as the military have to complete their duty often without question.

Much of what is read or reported in the media is critical, often unpatriotic or at the very least unhelpful. Yet my experience of this situation concerning the military is one of great care and organisation. When you actually look inside the enormous team of soldiers and back-up personnel that is essential to the system, you are left with a far better insight into the enormity of the problems faced by the military on a daily basis. I suppose that there will always be problems, shortages and, with hindsight, rethinks. But what large company of any kind would not find itself in the same position?

What has been a very pleasant surprise in meeting members of the military, from the lowest of ranks to the highest, is the dignity and respect that is shown to ourselves and the families we are all assisting. In my experienced view, that care has been excellent, and when we personally come under military care our security is paramount to them, great care indeed being taken of everybody who goes into that war zone. Naturally, I am apprehensive every time one of our staff or my family undertakes these tasks – who wouldn't be, going into such a situation? – but I am also extremely proud.

Countries such as Afghanistan or Iraq do not have a funeral system as we know it, or funeral directors to assist the military on site, something that you might have in a country like Germany, for instance. But it is inevitable that people are going to die, not just in action but often as a result of natural or accidental death, so provision has to be made. Going on one of these repatriation missions certainly opens your eyes to the extreme difficulties that are faced. The heat and obvious dangers, transport difficulties and of course some extreme weathers show you clearly just how difficult it is to adapt to and cope with such conditions.

Christopher himself attends most repatriations and is often accompanied by our staff: my son Simon, Jon Fletcher, Terry Card, Mark Richards, Michael Thorpe, Michael Gill and a number of others. In the future, that will probably include me too – as I always take my turn when it comes.

One of Christopher and Simon's recent trips was to

127

repatriate a journalist who had been killed near Baghdad. They flew off early one Saturday morning from Brize Norton in Oxfordshire on a TriStar jet to Basra. Upon landing in Basra, in temperatures of around 40–50 degrees Centigrade, they were transported on a Hercules plane to Baghdad. Receiving their luggage and equipment, they then headed off in an armoured car with a jeep convoy to a field hospital where the identification of the deceased, the preparation and the sealing of the coffin were completed.

When all was safely finished, and still under armed guard, they returned to Baghdad ready for a Hercules flight to Basra with the deceased. But then it was found that the Hercules had some kind of mechanical fault and needed a new part, causing the flight of course to be cancelled. Christopher and Simon had a considerable wait in the departure lounge, being well fed and cared for that day by the British armed forces, surrounded by the regulars and civilians waiting for hours for transportation to their various destinations. Unusually, in the end, Christopher, Simon and the deceased were taken aboard a Chinook helicopter kitted out with machine guns and a protection expert flying at quite a low level for their return to Basra. A fascinating but somewhat stressful trip.

During their journey, they flew across Babylon, that mystical city we have all heard of during our schooldays, famous throughout history for its Hanging Gardens. The helpful and very well-educated helicopter pilot kindly kept Simon and Christopher informed of the sights and the history, and of what speed and height they were travelling.

They eventually arrived in Basra only to find that they had missed their flight, meaning another delay, this time something like twelve hours spent at Basra Airport. At the airport,

128

little souvenir stalls and small shops have now mushroomed, selling old Saddam money, stamps of the realm, even small Republican Guard medals and shoulder epaulettes from the uniforms. It just underlines that wherever there are people, some sort of industry will grow from the current events.

Somewhere around Basra, Christopher had mislaid his glasses during a sandstorm. He decided that they must have actually blown off his face, but he could not find them anywhere. Amazingly, they later turned up with some of the deceased's personal effects that had been gathered and eventually returned to Christopher in London. Those glasses could really have been anywhere in Basra after that sandstorm, so for them to have been picked up and returned was really incredible.

Christopher and Simon eventually caught a TriStar flight back to Brize Norton and returned home after some four and a half days, extremely tired but very proud, as indeed was I. The deceased, of course, returned to Brize Norton too before being returned to his family. In many ways, families that have to cope with life after losing a son or daughter are themselves heroes. I am just proud to be part of what is a very sad but very necessary repatriation service, and all credit is due to the British military and to Christopher Henley for this incredible set-up, of which I am proud to be Chairman.

Having begun this unusual chapter with a poem from Rupert Brooke, I would like to end it with a poem from my own son Jonathan. It was written when he was a schoolboy between thirteen and fourteen years of age and, I think, depicts his fear of war and death as well as his amazing understanding of loss and the dreadful horrors of the First World War. I am of course biased, but I am very proud that he wrote it. It is called *No Man's Land*.

Dark, misty and damp
Without a light or lamp.
No bed to sleep in
No comfortable fire,
It's hard to sleep with all the barbed wire.
Death lurks in the air, the enemy seems everywhere.
Guns are firing, they would not stop,
The General ordered us over the top.
Each man stood for their Nation's pride
But in No Man's Land so many died.
The guns got louder, there were cries of pain
The slaughter continued through the pouring rain.
Then all that was heard was the dying breaths
Of countless young soldiers in this land of death.
So many died, some survived,
Some came home, barely alive.
Soldiers were crippled, some were blind,
Forever the memories will be in their minds.
Mothers and wives waited in vain,
For news of their loved ones they may never see again.
Tears were shed as the news was read
About those who served and now are dead.
From the war a lesson was learnt –
Respect for those who served was certainly earned.

Jonathan Dyer

In memory of all who have given their lives throughout
history so that people like me are *free* to write and
remember.

8

DEATH AND ITS SUPERSTITIONS

FOR SALE – SECOND-HAND HEADSTONE
WOULD SUIT FAMILY WITH THE
NAME OF MURPHY

Like putting new shoes on the table, having a second-hand headstone would probably be unacceptable (even if the original inscription suited us). Without us realising, superstition can play an enormous part in our daily lives. When involved with death, it is magnified a thousand times. Let's take a look at some of the superstitions I have heard of or come across during my career as a funeral director.

There are of course our local Cockney ones, which, even today, we are still careful not to break, for example the one I've already mentioned that if petals fall from the back of a hearse when it is leaving the cemetery (which is unacceptable and unforgivable), another funeral will be quick to follow. Similarly, red and white flowers should not be placed together because that represents blood and bandages.

There are others too. Immediately a death occurs in a house, or if a body is being returned to the house, all the mirrors must be covered to avoid reflections. This protects the past and the future, as the person who next sees their reflection in that mirror will be the next to die. Holding your collar, something frequently done by children, is said to avoid a death from fever. Today's children apparently have a new superstition of their own to deal with this – they hold their collars and then look for a four-legged animal to break the spell! We also avoid travelling through a tunnel at a funeral, the superstition being not to take anyone underground before their time.

I have heard of several more superstitions around Europe and North America. My old colleague Giovanni Primavesi from Italy informs me that many of the behaviours I describe below are commonly still regarded as superstitions, being feared and often respected by many of the cultures they have evolved from. You must hold your breath as you pass a cemetery or you are in danger of breathing in the spirit of someone who has died (that would be a problem if you were passing somewhere like Nunhead or Brookwood cemeteries – you would pass out before you were halfway along!). The spirit of someone who is buried in black is also said to return to haunt the family.

There are quite a few portents of death. Dreaming of a birth is said to signify an impending death (although dreaming of death is apparently a sign of certain birth). If a mirror should fall from the wall in a house and break, not only will it bring seven years' bad luck, but someone in the house will die shortly after. Dropping an umbrella on the floor means that there will be a murder in the house. Now, I have heard that opening an umbrella will bring much bad luck in a house, but leading to murder – well!

If a broken clock suddenly chimes, it is certain that it pronounces a forthcoming death in the family. But if someone has died, you must stop any clock in that room at the precise moment of death to avoid any future deaths there. (Come on now, make your mind up. Perhaps it would be better not to have any clocks in the house at all.)

Animals can be associated with death. A dog howling in the middle of the night means that there will be a death before daylight. A bird too is a sign of death – when it enters the house through a window, death will shortly follow, particularly if the bird is a robin, it seems (although what the robin has done to be so stigmatised, God only knows). White moths and butterflies do not fare much better: if they should try to enter the house, it also brings bad luck and a certain death.

Luckily, we can do a few things to protect ourselves. Lighting candles on the night after – *after*, remember – 1 November will protect your family for the coming year. Make sure that you do not sit thirteen people down at a table to eat or one of them will die before the year is over, a superstition no doubt coming from thoughts of Jesus' Last Supper. If three people are photographed together, the one in the middle will be the first to die. (So make sure you take three of each photo, shifting everyone round each time. In fact, if you can, never be the one in the middle.)

If none of these works and a death is about to occur, make sure that the soul of the dying person can escape – at the moment of death, all the windows in the room should be opened, and the locks in the house must be left undone so that the soul may be completely free to go to Heaven. If a dead person's eyes are left open, it is sure they will be looking for the next person to go with them. Apparently if the left eye twitches, there will soon be a death in the family. (What if the right eye twitches? And if they both twitch, perhaps you have been fooled and the person is not dead at all.)

It is said that a person who dies on Good Friday will go right to Heaven, and if you should die on the eve of Christmas, the Gates of Heaven are certain to be open for your entry. Superstition also has it that when a death occurs, a candle should be lit and placed in the window of the room: a lovely tribute, don't you think, even if we don't believe the superstition. And if you touch a loved one who has died, to say goodbye, they will always be in your heart and you will not have nightmares surrounding their death.

Funerals too are surrounded by superstition. Funerals on a Friday herald yet another death in the family later that year. Remember not to count the cars at a funeral – soon you could be counting the cars at your own (now that would be a miracle). It is bad luck to meet and block a funeral procession head on (that is certainly right, particularly if it is one of mine and you block my way). And pointing at a funeral procession will cause your own death by the end of the month. Nothing new should be worn to a funeral, especially new shoes; that would not go down well in Bermondsey as a new outfit is essential here. And pregnant women, superstition says, should not attend funerals (please, not in the last month anyway).

Even at this stage, superstition can give us an idea of what the deceased was like. Thunder following a funeral means a dead person has certainly reached the Gates of Heaven. If the person being buried has lived a good life, flowers will grow on the grave, but if the person was evil and lived a bad life, only weeds will ever flourish.

Last, one of my own sayings: 'If a horse passes wind at a funeral, it is certain that a second horse will respond, resulting in a rather unpleasant odour.' Well, I have to be a bit flippant – things can get too serious, and you could worry too much over superstitions and what might never happen.

You see, it is easy to make up a superstition from anything that might happen surrounding a death or at a funeral, but our whole lives are made up of rules and superstitions. They are the guidelines by which we walk through this world and perhaps even the guidelines that walk us into the next. You may be superstitious, you may not, but you have to admit that there are chains of events that are sometimes very strange. That's fate for you, I guess, always very unpredictable, but things always seem to pop up when you most need them.

Take what happened today, for instance. Here I was writing what some would say is a slightly spooky chapter when my publisher rang to talk about what the cover and photos would be like for this particular book. He asked for an old-fashioned picture to go in the book, but it had to be a picture we had not used before, either in previous books or for the television programme. I felt sure I did not have anything he had not seen already, but I said I would think about it and see what came up. Sure enough, when I looked through all my photos, I could find nothing.

Even though I had only really just started this chapter and should have been concentrating, I walked out of the office to get a cup of tea, running into a family we have served for many years.

'Oh Barry, I am so pleased I've seen you. I was saying to my daughter I was hoping we would see Barry. I've got something to show you,' and out came an envelope. Inside the envelope were three absolutely beautiful pictures of a horsedrawn funeral back in the early 1900s that I never knew existed.

''Ere y'are,' she said, 'take them and get copies for yourself. You are more than welcome.'

Well, I just couldn't believe it. I am always over the moon to see anything showing that kind of history or this firm, and I knew immediately that these pictures would be perfect for somewhere in the book. Ain't life the strangest thing – and death even stranger.

Now you read earlier the superstition about not having funerals on Fridays; well, how about having a funeral on Friday the thirteenth? That must be the ultimate of superstitions. I'm writing this chapter in mid-February 2004, and last week there was a Friday the thirteenth. We were very careful at our breakfast meeting (being a Friday, a big fry-up) to be sure that everyone was aware of the date and of the need to be extra careful that nothing should go wrong. We then left the funeral home on our way to our first funeral, at West London Crematorium, the funeral of a person who had been flown in from Eastern Europe to be cremated here. We turned left on to Jamaica Road, and directly in front of us was a cab. The badge number on the cab was 666 – the devil's number, or so superstition says. A good start, we thought.

When we arrived at the crematorium, four members of the family who were to attend the funeral were some fifteen minutes late. The sound equipment was not working, and part of the electricity in the chapel was turned off (fortunately, we had our usual in-house CD player on the hearse, batteries included). At the point of committal, the button was pushed, the doors at the back opened, and the coffin should have gone through. But it was an Eastern European coffin (with the metal removed, as you cannot cremate metal), which had slight legs on, and the legs had got caught and would not move on the roller. You could almost see the coffin going in and out, in and out, as it was getting caught and coming back again. Very spooky. The bier operation had to be halted immediately, and we explained the difficulty to the family. The four bearers then moved the coffin gently through by lifting. The family all understood and were very kind about the problem, but as we left the chapel they remarked, 'It is Friday the thirteenth, after all,' with a little chuckle.

On our way back, we witnessed two other number plates with 666 on. Then, as we pulled back into the yard, a bunch of flowers arrived some four hours late for that very funeral. I have to say that funeral had Friday the thirteenth written all over it. No one's fault; just a chain of superstition!

I guess everybody in our profession has a spooky story to tell. As you know, especially if you have read my first book, *Don't Drop the Coffin*, I am not short of a few myself. But I am not the only one to have had strange experiences here. Jon Fletcher, our Financial Director and a Director of F.A. Albin & Sons, also had a very strange encounter while having a cup of tea and a sandwich in our kitchen, which looks out on to our main yard. As he was drinking his tea and looking through the window daydreaming (as usual – ha, ha!), he noticed a very tall black gentleman pass the window. Thinking he was collecting or delivering something, Jon slipped out of the side door and through the garage in a matter of seconds, to where the gentleman should then have been standing. But he was nowhere to be seen, which was very strange because there was nowhere for him to disappear to. Jon called out, 'Is anyone there?' but there was no response. He looked around every nook and cranny, but there was nothing and no one to be found.

The only place left for this man to have gone was into the

mortuary, so Jon headed there. As he walked into the mortuary to ask David, one of our embalmers, whether he had heard or seen anybody, Jon saw, lying on the mortuary table awaiting preparation, the same very tall black man, identical in every way to the man he had seen walk past the window. Despite the fact that he is normally very level-headed and unshockable, a typical accountant you might say, shivers ran up and down Jon's spine. Even after six months, he is still convinced that he saw the very same man pass the window, and who can say? As you know, I believe that the soul lives on. Jon was convincing and I have to believe his story – I really do.

Another oddity we recently experienced was a strong smell of King Edward cigars in our reception, coming directly from the photo of Mr Ernie Albin in our 'Hall of Fame', as we call it. Strangely enough, these were his regular daily smoke and had a smell I will never forget. Joanna and Greg (our operational manager, who first joined us as a work experience boy some eight years ago) smelt it too, so it was not just my imagination.

It is always nice as a funeral director to have the opportunity to help someone who has perhaps helped you greatly in your life. It can of course sometimes also be a sad time, as it usually means that someone you know has passed away. This recently happened when my sons Simon and Jonathan's old headmaster died at home. What was unusual here was the way in which Maggie, his wife, came to contact us, the interesting view that her husband had of death, and some of the odd things that happened around her shortly after the funeral. I will let her tell the story in her own words, in the letter she wrote afterwards.

Dear Mr Albin,

You have no idea how you and Simon have helped me over the last few weeks. After the first episode of your programme, Ron was immediately on the phone to his friends boasting of his connection (reflected glory!) and telling stories of when he interviewed Simon and Jonathan for entry to Addeys. Your programme led us to talk about what kind of send off we wanted, and because of that I was able to give Ron that last favour (unconventional though it was). That would never have happened but for you.

The day after Ron died, the coroner rang me and said I should contact a local funeral director. I went up to Ron's study to look in Yellow Pages, and I found your book, half opened – Ron's current reading. I had no idea he had bought the book. Of course I immediately knew that he wanted you to do the honours.

This week I read your book – much to my sister's shock and horror! I think she was more astonished though at how I laughed out loud so many times. It has been a great comfort to me as well as a source of much entertainment, and I have now begun your second book, which is equally riveting.

The pride you have in your sons, from your book, is palpable and I can certainly see why. Simon was superb. What a credit he is to you.

I was very apprehensive of coming to the chapel to see Ron, and was even advised against it by some of my friends, but how glad I am that I did. It was wonderful to see him as he was. Whoever was responsible, my heartfelt thanks and admiration.

And Peter Fellows [the priest seen sleeping in the crypt with the deceased in Don't Drop the Coffin] – what a fantastic man he is. All my friends want to book him for their send off (though I don't think they want him to put it in his diary just yet!)

Many strange things have happened during the last few weeks, the most spectacular of which was the dining room ceiling crashing down when I was in Ron's study, asking him to show me he was near. Although neither of us are Christians, or even conventionally religious, we are certainly not atheists. I remember once Ron comparing death to an awakening. When you are dreaming, while you are in that dream, it is your life and everything in it is totally real and normal. It is only when you wake up from the dream that you realise you were dreaming. But sometimes, if the dream has been really beautiful, you lie there reliving it, almost wanting to be back in it, and you eventually get up and get on with your life, though you may at times, even years later, think about and relive the dream. On an infinitely larger scale Ron saw death as awakening from the dream of this life. But I think he has been lying there reliving the dream these past few weeks, and trying to get back into the dream! I think perhaps this is why the spirit/soul 'hangs around' for a while, and even may revisit in future when it thinks back to the dream. I hope so.

Well I will bring this to a close now, as I can hear myself rambling. I know there will be unbearable times ahead, but I will always look back on the day of the funeral as one of my wonderful memories.

Please pass on my sincere gratitude to your whole team, but especially Simon.
Maggie

I believe that there is so much truth in what Maggie says in her letter. I am sure that there is a connection between Ron's soul and the warmth of his presence around her. The narrow line that we walk between dreams and reality is in itself sometimes incredible.

It was clear from a second letter that Maggie wrote that the strange happenings had continued, making her more convinced than ever that Ron, or at least the warmth of his soul, is still around. Maggie says that she would love to meet up with me some time in the near future and tell me all the things Ron has done since he left. She says there is enough for a book itself! I personally think she is not just very brave but was also very much in love with Ron. The dead never leave us; they are a force that is always with us until our own dying day, when we may be at one.

Another kind lady who wrote to me after reading my book and watching the television series had also experienced some strange events in her home since her husband had died. Things going missing, which she felt he had helped her to find. Things being moved, and what she felt were interconnected messages being left for her in strange trails of coincidence. But perhaps the spookiest thing was that, only minutes after her husband's death, she took a photograph of him with a modern, very reliable camera containing a roll of film that had been half used over the previous weeks. She took just one photograph, but to her amazement, when the film returned from being developed, every photograph had come out quite clear and well focused –

except the one she had taken of her husband. There was nothing there at all. Very strange, but to this lady more comforting than frightening. She is a logical lady, not excitable or, you would think, susceptible to any kind of supernatural happenings, and she naturally wants to believe that her husband is still close to her. She is calm and understanding at the death of her husband but truly believes that his soul has never left her home. Who knows, perhaps she is right.

As we do with the superstitions I described above, we, as human beings, also read things into some of our other experiences. We see what we want to see and believe what we want to believe, and I am totally aware of that. But I am also very open to the importance of some of the events that surround funerals.

Releasing doves at a funeral has become very popular. Right at the end of the service, the priest might say a special prayer and we release a dove or a pair of doves to symbolise setting the soul free. At one particular funeral, at Honor Oak Crematorium, we released a dove at the end of the service, at about three o'clock on a late summer's afternoon. The doves always fly off into the sky and circle round to get their bearings before returning home, but on this occasion the dove just hopped into the nearest tree and then down on a colum-barium, where it simply sat watching us. It did not attempt to fly away at all. The family turned to each other and said, 'That's John for you; he just don't want to go. He wants to be here with us.' That brought an ease to the day and many contented smiles. The dove eventually flew into a nearby tree and we left the crematorium.

The next morning I was attending the exhumation of the wife of a dear old friend, Jim, at Camberwell New Cemetery.

We were then due to drive round to the Honor Oak Crematorium to undertake her final cremation, something her husband had planned for some time and which meant a great deal to him. He just felt he could not leave her there on her own in the cemetery: he wanted to bring the matter to a close with a cremation and be able to take her ashes home and keep her with him.

We completed the exhumation early that morning and drove round to the crematorium, where we were to meet Jim and his family. As we carried the coffin into the crematorium and placed it on the bier, the priest reading the words of farewell, I looked up as an unusual sound caught my attention. To my astonishment, the dove was sitting on the chandelier. Just as the coffin was lowered, the dove hopped into the catafalque, where it sat for a few moments before flying back to the chandelier. Jim and his family could not believe this symbolic presence. It was almost as if his dear late wife was saying goodbye and thank you in her own way, almost as if she were saying, 'This is what I wanted.'

Everybody was overwhelmed. The family left the crematorium that morning feeling so much better. What the dove had done was totally out of character. It had stayed there all night and gone into the chapel before the cremation that morning. At the moment of commitment, it had flown down from its perch on the chandelier for us all to see. You cannot tell me that this was not meant to be; I am sure it was more than just a coincidence. I am certainly glad that we were left with this lovely, endearing thought.

Afterwards, my boys and I went back to the chapel and, without too much difficulty, were able to retrieve the dove. It was almost as if it were saying, 'My work's done, let's go home now.' It still lives with us at Culling Road, quite happily sitting in our memorial garden, where it is planned that Jim will eventually bring his wife's ashes.

I had a strange experience myself at my local church. A lady whom I had never seen before approached me at the end of a funeral. She was gentle and petite, perhaps only five feet tall, with black frizzy hair, glasses and small teeth framed in a slightly fixed smile. Dressed in a long black coat and black hat, she spoke with an Eastern European accent. I remember clearly an unusual scent around her, a little like sulphur. Not the sort of person you would ever forget.

She told me that she had had a very strange feeling when she first saw me at the funeral Mass. She had lost her father in Poland many years before, when he was run over by a train, and had also, as a child, lost her mother as the result of a car accident. She told me that she saw in my face a compassion at her own loss such as she had never felt before. At the end of the Mass, as the priest, choir and congregation sang 'May the choirs of Angels come to greet you, may they speed you to Paradise' (which is sung at the end of every Mass at our local church), she had witnessed that I was clearly the Guardian of the passage that a deceased person takes from this life to the next.

She described that compassion as a gift, a presence that I had, and said that I was the only person in whom she had ever been able to truly see this. She felt I was the kind of Ferryman, protecting and leading not just the soul of the deceased whose funeral I was conducting, but also those of her parents. She was clearly serious and sincere, yet a little afraid as she saw something in or around me that she did not see in the priest, any of the staff or bereaved, or anyone around me. It was a little spooky for me but also, I guess, flattering.

I have never mentioned this experience to anyone, and I have not seen or spoken to that good lady since, but I must confess that this has troubled me somewhat. In one way, it is true, of course – it is a real gift and a big responsibility. On the other hand, thinking that I might never have a private moment, just me and my thoughts, is somewhat uncomfortable. Maybe I am being silly now. But it makes you think, doesn't it – how strange, how bizarre! It all caught me a little on the hop, but I still have a clear mental picture of this lady. She may no longer be part of this world herself, but if I do come across her again I am sure I will have a few questions to ask her.

Another person I seem to have had a marked effect on is Jenny, a lovely local lady in her early forties, who, it would be fair to say, has been very connected with death itself. She is one of the kindest ladies I have ever come across around Bermondsey, always helping those who have lost loved ones. Very generous, she would do anything for anyone. She is, however, also very nervous and excitable around a death and has had bereavement close around her recently, having lost many of her own family over the past few years.

At twelve o'clock on this particular day, we were due to bring the deceased home, where he was to lie for three days before the funeral. We pulled up at 11.55 outside the house, and the boys began to prepare the 'going home equipment' – crucifix, candlesticks, etc. – then moved them from the vehicle in preparation. I quietly knocked at the door. After about twenty seconds, the door opened and there was Jenny, looking straight at me. I was about to say, 'Morning, Jenny,' when she screamed, grabbed her hair and threw her arms up in a total panic. I was as afraid as I have ever been around any spooky events, I can tell you. It was really unnerving.

Jenny just continued to scream, and I had to look behind me in case there was something dreadful there that was frightening her. This state of affairs seemed to go on for ages as Jenny was jumping up and down in total nervous panic. Eventually, her family came running out and grabbed her, trying to calm her down. And within a moment she was fine.

'Barry,' she said, 'I am so sorry.'

'But Jenny, you knew I was coming at twelve; what was wrong?'

She replied, 'I don't know. I opened the door and there was Barry.'

'Yes, and . . . ?'

'Well, that was it, it just spooked me, really spooked me, because I was thinking "Barry" and I opened the door, and there you were.'

To this day, we still laugh over that event. 'I don't know what came over me,' Jenny said. 'I can see now the logic of what you were saying, but I was just spooked, totally spooked. I thought "Barry" and there you were in front of me, and for a moment it was like I was in a dream.'

I said, 'That's all right Jenny . . . but you frightened the life out of me too.'

Quite another kettle of fish is the brother of Elaine from our Deptford branch. He is a very talented hairdresser and has on occasion looked after the deceased's hair when Jackie or Elaine has not been available, especially when it is a friend or relative. On this particular occasion, while he was working on a lady's hair, her hands, which were clasped across her chest, just slipped apart and shook the life out of him. Terrified, he had to sit down, have a cup of tea and get his nerves back together again.

I just smiled: 'Well, that happens sometimes, Gary.'

'Not to me, it don't,' he replied.

He had a point, of course – to me, it was not so terribly unusual, but Gary's everyday customers are alive, so he was not expecting this.

So there we are. We have had a close look at the strange, the spooky, the superstitious, the strange moments that surround death itself. I want to finish with something quite natural but nevertheless very funny and really lovely. Returning to one house at the end of a funeral, there was a kind of a strange silence in the living room where the daughter sat with her mum, reflecting on the events of the day. The mum suddenly turned to her daughter and said, 'What would Dad want us to do now, darling, if he were here?'

The daughter looked at her and replied, 'Mum, he would want us to dig him up, of course.'

'Course he would, wouldn't he? . . . What am I saying? What's the matter with me?'

'Nothing, Mum, you just miss Dad like we all do, but I'm with you and that's not going to change.'

Bless her. What a lovely girl.

9
WHAT? A NEW FLEET?

It could be said there are many good reasons for an individual to own a hearse, remembering of course that if it is a Rolls-Royce hearse, it will never break down – just occasionally fail to continue. You could buy a Rolls Can-Hardly, probably quite cheap because it rolls down the hills but can hardly get up them, but what good practical reasons are there for somebody to own a hearse?

Well, it has more than enough leg-room, of course. And it is certainly easy to find in a parking lot. At a crowded intersection, people might well pull over, giving you right of way, such is the habit of respect for such a vehicle. In the winter, you can put your skis inside on the bier – you won't have to strap them on the roof any more. And for the first time in your life, you might also meet people who are stranger than you are – you would probably be considered a bit weird because you are driving a hearse as a private vehicle, and that would be sure to attract some oddballs.

You would not have to buy a fold-up bicycle to beat the

Central London congestion charge. You could just whip your bike out from under the bier when you reached the ever-expanding edge of the zone. Some would say it was also the perfect vehicle for passion. For use as a travelling hotel, my dad and I have certainly found the ground floor perfect accommodation (remember my trip to Wales as a little lad, described earlier in the book). And at the very end, of course, you could save money, because rather than burying it one day, it could bury you. A hearse is far less likely to be stolen, too, and I would until recently have said that it is far less likely to be car-jacked – but then I heard this true story from Iraq.

It seems that an armed gunman ordered at least ten mourners and a deceased person from the back of a makeshift hearse that they were using to take a member of their family to be buried. The car-jacker sped off in the hearse, leaving the mourners and the body literally on the road in the desert. The funeral party were eventually picked up by an American patrol who then kindly took them and the deceased to the cemetery and assisted with the burial. Comforting to think that if you get car-jacked, some well-meaning person will come along and assist you.

All said and done, a hearse would not be such a bad all-round vehicle for the average motorist. And, joking aside, a hearse is – after the coffin, of course – one of the most essential tools of the funeral practice.

The history of the hearse has been well documented in many other books. My earliest memory of a hearse is of the high-bred Rolls-Royce vehicle that we still have today, and its sister hearse, identical in almost every way, which I recently recovered for Albin's from my dear old friend Taslim Ali, who obtained it when he bought a business in North London. That particular hearse, although too dilapidated to be restored, is still serving a purpose, as it has been used as a pattern for my new hearses, which are being hand-built for us in Doncaster. These new hearses will include the windows of our old hearse and its beautiful cut-glass side windows. The lovely old bier and seats, the side flower rails and of course the whole body of this second hearse will be used as a mould, at least for the rear half of the new vehicles.

We had lost ownership of the hearse I recovered when it was sold back in the 1960s. Having an old crash gearbox and poor steering circle, it was becoming difficult to use for funerals, so it was sacrificed when we bought a new fleet of Van den Plas vehicles. The other hearse, however, stayed with us through the years. Back in the mid-1990s, I had it completely renovated to the beautiful standard and condition that it still maintains today. It is an absolute picture and my pride and joy. The chassis is dated 1932, with bodywork built in 1951/2. It is the most reliable vehicle I have ever known and, I sincerely hope, the one that will take me on my last journey – eventually. It is so beautifully made that it will certainly outlive me.

Whenever I have a good idea for adapting a hearse, I usually find that, somewhere along the way, it has already been done. At one time, I thought of having a hearse that had the mourners in it as well, but, after some consideration I came to the conclusion that people generally prefer to be separate from the deceased on their final journey. As you can imagine, I was more than surprised when, thinking that this was an original idea, I came across an old advert for Chelsea Carriage Works Limited, a company in West London that used to convert vehicles into hearses. The advert, dating from the early 1900s, was for the 'Chelcar triple purpose saloon hearse mounted to Austin 20 H.P. four cylinder chassis built by the oldest and most up to date firm of coach builders in the undertaking trade, Chelsea Carriage Works Limited'. The lovely old-fashioned picture showed the following:

Ten special features of the Chelcar triple purpose saloon hearse:

1 all exterior woodwork and panelling in eighteen gauge aluminium;
2 detachable child's glassette taking a four-foot coffin [that's a small bier covered in glass for a child's funeral];
3 invisible rear door [for the Invisible Man, no doubt];
4 comfortable seats for six mourners, conductor and driver;
5 bier space of six feet ten inches up to glass partition – a seven foot six inch box can be carried by lowering the partition glass;
6 private locks to all doors;
7 two adjustable ventilators in roof [absolutely essential in those days as there was often quite an aroma];
8 absence of moulding, thereby eliminating chipped paint-work [don't ask me about that one];
9 no overhanging at rear of body [the vehicle body, of course];
10 a waterproof [no less!] V-shaped windscreen.

So in the very early 1900s, we are already looking at an all-in-one, dual-purpose vehicle hearse and limousine.

At the other end of the scale, a funeral journal advertised as recently as 2003 a hearse with some 'unique' features, but not so unique that they had not been thought of or used before. There was a side window that opened on a hinge so you could have full side access to the coffin and the flowers that could be laid alongside or on top of it. A brilliant new idea, except that this was exactly the kind of side window that the Victorian funeral director would have had on his horse-drawn hearse. What about the secret door that opens like a box, allowing you easy access to the space underneath the bier, where much of your equipment can be stored? Again, every Victorian horsedrawn carriage had such a box just under the driver's seat. The side flower rails to hang and lay the flowers against were yet another essential on the horsedrawn equivalent. Another idea was creating bearers' seats by flipping down a piece of the bier. This derived from early motor hearses and is a prominent feature of both of our old hearses.

So, you see, not much is really new in this world, and this applies as much to our own industry as it does to every other one. I personally have never been attracted by the supersonic styling of hearses or funeral vehicles. I much prefer something classic and timeless, which is what we have tried to achieve in creating our own personalised fleet. Many prominent people in the funeral industry have told me I am taking a really big gamble in following such a route, but I prefer to think of it as a calculated risk. It is certainly not the easy route to go, that's for sure. It would be far simpler to get a purpose-made Daimler, Mercedes, Ford, Vauxhall, Volvo, that kind of motor fleet, but this would not set us aside from anyone else, nor would it give us that timeless, elegant, classic look.

You might be thinking: why not go the Rolls-Royce route if you want that? To do that, I would have to buy 1980s Rolls-Royce saloons and pay a small fortune to have them converted to limousines and hearses. I would then effectively end up with twenty-year-old vehicles, classic but not really timeless, that are, in my opinion, not built for day-to-day work. The cost of ordering a brand new fleet directly from Rolls-Royce would be totally unmanageable, and therefore not an option, although I would love a fleet like the new Bentley that has been purpose-built for the Queen. What an outstanding vehicle – upright, elegant, classic, timeless, yet full of today's technology – just the kind of vehicle that I want. So the only way to achieve my aim is to have a vehicle hand-built to my specification that will fulfil all my requirements. And that is exactly what I intend to do.

I have never taken the easy road in life, and I am not going to start now! In reality, honest achievement comes, as they say, from about twenty per cent inspiration and eighty per cent perspiration. Being hands-on is the only way for me, but of course I have a little help from my friends – Steve Ali, Martin Green and the incredible Fred Albin, all three of them, in my opinion, experts around vehicles.

There isn't a vehicle that Steve Ali has not driven or worked on over the years, and, having had a lifetime in the funeral industry, I have to respect his knowledge. Martin is exactly the same, having run a fleet of fifty or more cars with his father for a number of years. There is not much that he cannot do with or to a motor car. Fred, of course, has spent his life being a kind of father to me, but has also had the experience of designing hearses over the years and has great engineering ability. With a little modern input from my two sons and financial control as always from Jon Fletcher, I reckon we have a winning team. Add to this a little advice from my old friend Freddie Collins, another driving and motoring wizard, and the risk is, in my opinion, completely calculated.

I am also supported by my mechanic Kenny. Any who know him will know that he is a master of two languages – Cockney English and out-and-out profanity, of which he is a master second to none. But what a mechanic! He is the kind of guy who can take an engine, strip it to bits, spread it across the floor, jumble it all up and find a way to put it all back together so that it works perfectly. He is truly gifted; it is just that he has never been blessed with etiquette and good language!

I had the good fortune to be introduced, through Martin Green, to the Vintage Motor Company and Alan Seilby. I noticed in his brochure that he had the rights to build a car called a Royale, a hand-built vehicle based on an old 1950s-style touring car. For the first time, I had seen a car whose basic lines were exactly right, but could this be redesigned and built into limousines and hearses – a truly enormous task? What followed on from my discovery was a number of meetings with Alan and his staff. Fred and I got busy doing small line drawings, and I cut out pictures of the Royale and pieced them together with paste. I had to get a final vision of what might be. Alan came down and took pictures and looked at our Rolls-Royce, once owned by the Sultan of Brunei, and with goodwill all round we struck a deal.

I agreed initially to pay for the tooling – half of it, anyway – with Alan. So balance paid and contracts signed in June 2003, the project began in earnest. By the end of November, we had a stuck-together rolling chassis to go and see at the lovely factory in Doncaster. In late November, I took all the men from work up so that they would all have an opportunity to take part in the project in some way. I insisted, of course, that Kenny came with us.

It was a Saturday, which meant that Kenny would miss his Saturday lunchtime drink – and he was none too happy about that. We travelled by train, arriving at Doncaster station in the late morning. Alan and his lads picked us up in several vehicles and took us to the factory. There in the showroom window of the factory was the rolling chassis, far from perfect in its grey primer, far from the finished article, but a first vision of what might be. For my sons and me, this was quite a moving moment. We were like bees around a honey pot. We were in the car, out of the car, underneath the car. It was all very exciting.

But the funniest moment of the day came when Kenny lifted up the bonnet to see . . . no engine or any mechanical bits whatsoever. I am sure you can imagine the first words out of his mouth (I hope you will excuse my language here).

''Ere,' said Kenny, 'there ain't no f****** engine 'ere, there ain't no f****** gear box, no f****** axle, no f****** suspension. In fact, there's f*** all for me to look at.'

'But Kenny,' I said, 'you are part of the team. Come on, mate, enter into the spirit.'

'F*** the spirit. I've wasted my f****** time coming today.'

'No you haven't, Kenny,' I replied. 'We'll go upstairs now and look at some of the engines that might be going in it.'

'I could have done that on the f****** phone.'

Everyone was in tears of laughter because he was so wound up, and just at that moment out came Alan's wife with a pot of tea and biscuits.

'Oh,' retorted Kenny, 'f****** handsome. It was worth coming just for the tea and biscuits.'

He never spoke to me all the way home, but at least we can laugh about it now.

Martin and I made our second visit to the factory in late December. This time, the changes discussed at our first visit had been completed, and the vehicle was almost as we wanted it to be. With just a few minor alterations to the shape of the back window and the height of the bonnet, we would have the mould that we wanted.

But being classic, beautiful and elegant is in itself not enough. The Albin Royale, as it will be named, has to have modern and prestigious technology and some unique features. For example, the front seat will be a bench seat, something that was commonplace in years gone by but is no longer seen today; it just gives you that extra bit of room and more comfort. It will be a four-door limousine with the unique feature of two hidden doors, making six when required. When I say hidden I mean that they will not have door handles but electric releases operated by the chauffeur. So when we need easy entry, we can convert to six doors, yet we have the stylish and classic look of a four-door limousine.

The back seats, again two bench seats, will be facing each other so that families can sit and have a face-to-face conversation on their way to the funeral – what in modern terms we call conference seating. Nothing new here, though; this was a standard arrangement in all horse-and-carriages in years gone by: people always sat facing each other. But we hope to introduce a very different take on this. The bench seat that is situated behind the driver will be capable of swivelling round, so that if a family have had a dispute and are not talking to each other (which sometimes happens) they need not face each other. There are also those people who feel sick when they are travelling with their back towards the engine, in which case we will be able to spin the seat round, operate the additional doors for an easy entry and easy exit, and there you have it – total versatility.

We have addressed other areas too. The boot will open outwards, rather than upwards, and on ratchets, so, for a very large funeral, extra bunches can if necessary be placed in the boot to make a fine display. There will of course be a huge roof rack for flowers and, on the bonnet, our own unique Nymph Flying Lady, which is being designed especially for us. The car will have sweeping wings and running boards.

So the car will be efficient, environmentally friendly, comfortable yet modern in its technology. It will of course have lovely woodwork, beautiful Axminster carpeting, first-class leather, air-conditioning, music systems (in case a family want to listen to something special), satellite navigation, literally everything one could want in a car. There will be a very prestigious engine, gearbox, running gear and suspension, all of which are still being chosen. If I get this right, it will be the most classic and beautiful car available. If I get it wrong, it will be a disaster, but I'm sticking to the old adage of 'He who dares, wins'.

As I write this, in March 2004, we are making the final decisions on the style of the hearse, based, as I have already said, on our old high-bred Rolls. It should be a real beauty. That finally decided upon, all the parts will be ordered. With moulds completed, production will begin probably in May 2004, to be completed by the start of 2005. A completely new fleet and, I hope, the finest in the land.

As further models are sold in the future, the tooling costs will be repaid and a new era of limousines and hearses will have begun, even if much of it has derived from the past. People in South London, particularly Bermondsey, will be the first to test these newly evolved vehicles – not that they will be queuing up to get into them, of course. Funeral vehicles are usually the last anybody wants to ride in.

You may wonder why I am going to so much trouble to create such a vehicle. After all, modern factory-built stretch limousines and hearses will surely carry some status. I agree that that is true, and many people will not mind whatever the vehicles look like; to Albin's and to me, however, it will always matter. We have to strive to continue being the very best. Everybody who rides in a hearse, either upright or horizontal, is the most important person in the world for a moment. Although some will say that 'a car is a car, what the hell?', many more will want the very best!

How about the lovely lady who asked me, when I was talking to some old friends in Moe Stevens Jewellers in the Blue, "Ere Barry, 'ow much is your 'orse and cart?"

I told her, of course.

'Oh lovely. Thanks, Bal. I want to know 'cos me mum's gonna want one of em,' and off she trotted.

As she left, my friends turned to me, laughing: ' " 'Orse and cart" she called it, Barry. A beautiful Victorian horse-drawn carriage, not an 'orse and cart.' Well, I knew exactly what she meant. That's just what endears me to Bermondsey people – they say it as it is. No airs and graces. Just like they used to call buses 'charabangs'. I love Bermondsey – I really do.

Even the new funeral ambulances I have just ordered will be uniquely special. They will of course be in our colours, with all the lettering in black and gold. They will be environmentally friendly too. They will carry all the correct equipment but, most importantly, they will have hydraulic rise-and-fall biers: at the push of a button, the bier will be lifted into the air, making room for four special trolleys. Because of our international shipping business, we receive caskets and crates containing human remains from all over the world, so to make it as easy as possible for the staff, the biers are to be extra long, a minimum of nine feet, making it simpler to put a coffin or crate on them when they have been completely lowered. Everything we do is thought out to the smallest detail. We have to strive for perfection in what we do.

From the back-room equipment through to what families see every day, it should make no difference. What is behind the scenes must be as good as what you see with your own eyes. We have a sign fixed to the staff mirror that says, 'Are you dressed correctly for Albin's? What you see in the mirror, the family sees. Have pride in yourself.' And to a person, they truly do.

We have now added an old blue sock, with the statement: 'Be sure to remove all blue socks from your black sock drawer to prevent a mix-up.' It would be unacceptable for us to wear blue at a funeral. Like anyone else, we will never be perfect, but we will never stop trying.

I guess that, since Man invented the wheel, he has created specialist vehicles for carrying deceased people, which we call hearses. In the earliest days, a plain two-wheeled cart was used. That was developed into a four-wheeled cart, which then evolved into a cart pulled by an animal – a horse, a mule or a donkey. In various countries around the world, all kinds of working animal would pull such a vehicle.

Boats such as gondolas, barges and houseboats have all been converted into hearses. There has been every kind of motor hearse you could imagine, from the oldest of hearses, which we used to call chocolate boxes because that's what the back of the hearse looked like, to the most modern, streamlined, aerodynamic vehicles that are available today (just what we are trying to avoid at Albin's!). There are motorbike hearses with sidecars that carry the coffin, and trailers that are pulled with the coffin on them. There are even air hearses in America, aeroplanes that act specifically as hearses. Not to be forgotten, of course, is the train that had its own coffin boxes in carriages for the bereaved and mourning, just like the mourning train that toured America carrying the body of Abraham Lincoln all over the US before his burial. So whatever kind of new futuristic vehicle Man devises, he will also come up with an idea to convert it to a hearse.

So what next? A skateboard hearse, or maybe a roller-skate hearse? There is certainly a sledge hearse that exists over in Canada. Maybe somewhere even a hovercraft. Fascinating, isn't it, when you get down to it? Man can be so inventive in life and death. And let's not forget the three-wheeler 'Del Boy' hearse that still lives in North London. Even a submarine can become a hearse: I seem to remember James Bond being shot from one of the cylinders of a submarine for a burial at sea. Who knows what the future will hold? Could you imagine Kenny, in a diving suit, servicing an Albin's submarine? The air bubbles would be full of foul language.

As well as being vital to the funeral business, hearses can of course be quite dangerous, particularly for the funeral director or conductor who is walking in front. If the hearse driver takes his eyes off you for one moment and you stop, the next minute you are under the bonnet. That nearly happened last year to my son Jonathan, conducting a funeral, when Perry momentarily glanced sideways to where some people were standing. Unfortunately, he did not notice that Jonathan had stood still to remove his hat out of respect, expecting that Perry would immediately stop too. But he didn't, and he ran into the back of Jonathan's knees, causing him to go down on all fours. It only takes a moment's loss of concentration. Perry will *never* forget that incident, I can promise you that – bless him!

Walking backwards in front of a hearse when you are

guiding it out of a turning can also be quite dangerous, as I found out when, to everyone's amusement, I once inadvertently walked into the back of a lorry. But luckily hearses are not always as dangerous, more often being helpful, as we found one late evening at a South London cemetery where the grave for the burial had not been dug correctly. We had to put the hearse's headlights on to illuminate the area of the grave so that the grave-diggers could see well enough to continue digging. You just never know what is going to happen. A funeral director's lot is sometimes anything but a happy one.

There is an old saying among funeral directors: 'Either I am dead or my watch has stopped – which is it?' You see, we are never late, just occasionally slightly in front or occasionally slightly behind. We can, however, sometimes have tunnel vision as we become so immersed in our work that we sacrifice our personal lives. If you are reading this, Simon and Jonathan, that it is not a good idea, but I think you already know that. I guess everybody has at some time looked at a funeral director and wondered whether he was dead or alive. I like to look at the *Bermondsey and Southwark News* every week, and I am always greatly relieved when I cannot find my name in the obituary notices. Mind you, if the new fleet does not work out, I might yet find my name in an obituary notice buried somewhere among the dead vehicles.

10

ANYTHING CAN (AND
USUALLY DOES) HAPPEN

The *Sunday Mirror* newspaper recently reported how one funeral descended into chaos after the mourners began brawling. Wreaths were sent flying, and the funeral director's car windows were smashed outside the Bushbury Crematorium in Wolverhampton. Staff locked the coffin inside the crematorium, and the service took place with a police guard after the rowing mourners had left. You see, anything can happen.

Grief can often bring the worst out in people, and I am sure every funeral director has heard the funny/sad jokes that surround funerals and death: 'It is not the cough you're coughing, it's the coffin they carry you off in.' Or 'The coffin rolled out the back of a hearse and down a hill straight into a chemist shop, and the man sat up and said, "Have you got anything to stop this coffin?" '

Then there is the one about the funeral that was proceeding down the high street followed by a man with a dog and behind him hundreds of other men. A man watching from the kerb turned to the man next to him and said, 'What's that all about?'

'Well,' said the second man, 'it seems that the man with the dog is the husband of the lady in the hearse.'

'Really? What happened?'

'Well, the man came home from work to find that the dog had savaged his wife.'

'Oh no! That's terrible, isn't it?'

Then the man thought for a few moments and said, 'Here, do you reckon there's any chance of me borrowing that dog?'

'Yeah,' the other fella said, 'you probably could, but you'd better get in the queue behind the other men who are following the funeral.'

We of course hear the ridiculous shouts of 'Don't drop the coffin' and 'Have you got any empty boxes, mister?' from the kids we pass. The humour poked at funerals and death seems to be endless. In the end, it is all part of everybody's individual fear of death itself, but humour sometimes comes from what is said or written without thinking. For example, on the gates of one cemetery it is written 'Only dead people living here may be buried'. What it really means, of course, is that you must live in the parish in order to qualify to be buried here when you are dead, but it does not sound that way, does it? On the gates of one of our local crematoriums, the council's badge is displayed: 'All's well done here' – well, that's no less than you would expect! It is of course depicting the council standard that the staff will act properly at all times, but again it does not come over like that. 'All's well done here' would certainly have an interesting extra meaning on the gate of a crematorium.

One of our families recently prepared a tape of a piece of music that they wanted to be played at the funeral. I always like to have a tape or a CD well in advance of the funeral so I can test it all out, but on this occasion it was presented to us just before we went into church, minutes before in fact, so we had no chance at all to try it out. The family, however, had assured us that it was ready to go. The piece of music they had chosen was from the opera *Tosca*, but they had taped it over some 'garage music' on a tape provided by the son. Somehow or other, the tape had double-tracked, so as we were walking in with the coffin, what we heard was the interesting combination of *Tosca* backed by garage. Luckily, the family liked it so much that they wanted it played again as we left the church.

I once visited a funeral home in San Antonio, Texas, owned by a huge American character called Fred. Huge in every way – stature, personality, voice. San Antonio is very close to the Mexican border, and this particular funeral home cared mostly for Mexican families living in that area, as well as employing Mexican staff. Fred took me around the funeral home, which was really quite impressive – very Catholic and very Mexican, as you would expect. I started to go into one of the chapels to have a look, but the door was locked.

'No, Barry,' he said, 'I keep the doors locked.'

'That's interesting,' I said.

'Well,' he said 'I have to.'

'Why is that?' I enquired.

'Well, if I didn't, I would have the staff screwing around in the chapels and, man, I'm not going to have that.'

'Oh, don't be awful,' I said, 'that can't be true; you are definitely exaggerating, Fred.'

'You think so?' he said and shouted, 'Maria!' Out came Maria.

'Maria, why do I keep these doors locked?'

You can imagine my embarrassment at this, but without a second thought, she simply said, 'Well Fred, we can't have the staff screwing around on the premises so, no problem, we keep them locked.'

I must confess I was a little shocked by those revelations, but Fred then showed how caring he is in his work, saying, 'Almost every funeral we have here, we hire an off-duty police motorbike outrider so that the funeral moves nicely through and there is a respectful procession.' This would be a great idea in the UK. In fact, I wrote to Ken Livingstone, the Mayor of London, about it earlier this year, but I have not yet had a reply.

Last year, we had a funeral of a local dustman who had done quite well for himself from his retirement pension and had invested it wisely. This gentleman, a dustman all his life, had purchased the Rolls-Royce belonging to the actor Stanley Holloway, who played a dustman in the film *My Fair Lady*. On the day of the funeral, the man's son drove their Rolls-Royce behind our 1932 Rolls-Royce hearse, in between our Sultan of Brunei's 1990 Rolls-Royce limousine and the following cars. What a lovely tribute. And when we got to the cemetery, what did we come out to? You've got it – 'My Old Man's a Dustman'. Everybody joined in and sang; it was an absolutely fantastic occasion. Tears, laughter and a little apt jollification. On the way back, we – naturally – played a tape of Stanley Holloway singing 'With a Little Bit of Luck'. Stanley Holloway was in fact quite famous for songs about funerals. There was 'My Word, You Do Look Queer' ('queer' meaning not well) and 'Brown Boots at a Funeral, I Ask You', songs I learnt as a child from my mum, my dad and Fred. He was a real Cockney character, Stanley Holloway, no doubting that.

Another real character is Joey, one of our local 'jack the lads', who came to see me recently. 'Bal, have I got stuff for you or what, mate. Tailor-made quality coats. I bought them all from a hire firm closing down. Beautiful mourning suits, Barry. Suit you down to the ground, and cheap; you've never had it so good.'

'All right, Joey, get them out,' I said. 'Let's have a look. Now you are telling me the truth that you bought them from a hire place?'

'Bal, went to a sale yesterday; the firm's closed down and I've got the gear.'

'Now you wouldn't tell me different, would you, Joe?'

'Bal, would I be in here if it was any different?' and he put his hand out to shake in honesty.

I shook his hand back and took on that honesty, because with Bermondsey people you can do that. A true Bermondsey handshake is as straight as an oak and just as strong.

So in comes Joey, and I open up the zip-up bag.

'Lovely mourning coat,' I said.

'Lovely mourning waistcoat,' I said.

'Lovely stripes,' I said.

'Beautiful cravat,' I said.

'Bal, what did I tell you? I'd never let you down, would I?'

'Perfect, Joe. Perfect for a bloody wedding, not a bloody funeral. It's all wedding hire, not funeral hire. The only thing any good at all would be the coats, and they're too short.'

'No, Bal, you're having a laugh,' he said. 'I thought it was all hire gear.'

'Well, it is all hire gear, but it's wedding hire gear not funeral hire gear. In fact, you would have quite a job hiring stuff for a funeral.'

'Oh, come on, Bal. Take it anyway. It's dirt cheap, and you can use the jackets, can't you? And look at them stripes. If you all had the same, they would look lovely.'

'Yes,' I replied, 'they wouldn't look bad, Joe, and I suppose I could have a couple of the jackets altered.'

So I bought three of them, mostly to keep Joey happy, and put them away. They will come good one day, and as for Joey, he was well pleased with his day's work.

Something that I never thought I would see occurred only a few weeks ago when I was driving along with a funeral cortège of four cars in the East End. I was on the inside lane when a second funeral passed me, doing about twenty-eight miles an hour while I was proceeding at a sedate sixteen or eighteen miles an hour. I was a little bit shocked and a little disappointed that such a thing should happen. In my dad's day, so he tells me, it was unheard of for one funeral to pass another. I think that the conductor, who caught a glance at my face and then immediately looked in the opposite direction, saw that I was not amused.

Looking through some magazine archives last week, I came across a short but interesting article, also on traffic, published in the funeral directors' journal back in 1929, so that all funeral directors would, I guess, take heed or be at the ready. The article is called 'Causes of Motor Accidents', and I quote:

The following analysis was recently made in a large city in the UK August 1929:

High speed caused 35.7 per cent of the accidents. High speed resulted in accidents when drivers were speeding 20 ft highway; when passing from a harder surface on to a softer surface; when making a sharp turn; or when approaching bridges.

Neglecting of signal rules, 3.5 per cent. This percentage is the result of drivers failing to signal to cars in the rear, when making a left turn on the highway.

Bursting of rear tyre, 3.5 per cent
Repairing tyre on highway, 5.3 per cent
Collision at cross roads, 3.5 per cent
Careless driving, 15.9 per cent. In several instances the driver was looking behind, and in one instance the driver was asleep.

Broken steering rods, 3.5 per cent
Blinded by bright lights, 3.5 per cent
Cutting in, 3.5 per cent
Hit from the rear, 1.7 per cent
Striking against kerb, 3.5 per cent
Running into farmer's wagon, 1.7 per cent
Unknown causes, 13.5 per cent

I think that the message here, as far as the funeral director is concerned, is the actual number of deaths on the road as opposed to their cause. Our professional associations like us to be fully informed, you know, but, as a funeral director I dislike undertaking a funeral for someone whose life has been brought to a premature close by such an accident. I would much rather wait politely for people to die naturally.

When people know that you are a funeral director, there are always so many questions they want to ask you. In general that is fine, and I am happy to answer them, but on holiday, as somebody who finds it very hard to relax anyway when I am away from the business, I have taken a conscious decision not to tell people what I do for a living. With that in mind, Jackie and I booked seven days for a quiet break in the Caribbean in the latter part of 2003. We both said that we were not going to tell anybody what we did for a living, and in fact that we would not get involved in any kind of friendship or conversation, but just chill out and relax if we could. This we really did try to do, but a number of people approached us at the airport and while we were dining out in the Caribbean just to say how much they had enjoyed the television programme and just wanted to say hello. They were really nice about it, not at all stressful, I have to say.

One afternoon, however, we were sitting by the pool relaxing. We were both reading when an American couple sat down just opposite us and said, 'We're going to get a drink; would you like one?'

We thanked them and shared a drink with them, and then they started to chat about the resort and what they had been doing. Inevitably, the conversation came round to what we did for a living. Jackie just said, 'Well, I help Barry,' and I said, 'I write books' (which of course I now do!).

'That's interesting,' they said. 'What about?'

'About life and death,' I said, hoping that they would think there was not too much difference between the two.

'That's really interesting,' said the man and began to tell me about his fascinating work in the oil business.

Then his wife turned to us with a real New York accent and said, 'Hey, ya know, ya look like kind people and ya sound like kind people. I would have said you're the sort of guy who worked with people.'

'Smart,' I thought.

'Me,' she said, 'that's what I do. I'm a funeral director, ⸱d-generation Italian.'

⸱here you are, the only two people we spoke to at any

length in the whole of the holiday, and by a vast coincidence she happened to be in a family funeral business (following her father), her son also working with her. At that point, I had to confess. 'I don't just write books. We're both funeral directors too,' and we told her why we had kept our profession secret. We all had a great laugh, exchanged stories and enjoyed the moment. How amazing to go all that way just to run into someone else from the other side of the world who does exactly what you do. That lovely lady (what a character too!) still keeps in touch with us by e-mail.

Another holiday we spent with my old friend Steve Ali and his wife Kelly. We went on one of those boats that go around the Turkish isles. It was a great week, quite relaxing, beautiful weather and lovely swimming. There were ten other people on the boat, and we decided that, because all four of us are funeral directors, we would not tell anyone what we did. All we said was, 'We're not going to tell you, you are going to have to guess.' We got through the whole week without them really guessing or us confessing. I am not sure what I will do the next time somebody asks me when I am on holiday. Once you have been on television for six weeks, on a programme probably seen by about forty million people overall, it might be better to tell the truth, keep your head down and get on with it. On the whole, though, people are lovely, aren't they? Very kind and interesting to talk to. But when you work in a service industry like this and you spend every day working with and for people, it is nice to chill out and not have to talk if you do not want to.

Steve, a larger-than-life character whom I absolutely love to death, once borrowed my two sons for an evening job with his hearse to assist with the bearing. On their way back with the hearse, Steve noticed that he was a bit short of petrol; in fact he was on reserve and could not have had any less. So he pulled straight into the petrol station and filled up, then noticed that right next to the petrol station was a McDonald's. Yes, you've guessed it: around goes Steve with the hearse through the drive-in – 'Four Big Macs to go, please.' Simon and Jonathan could not get over the fact that Steve would take a hearse in like that.

But Steve was not being disrespectful; his work was done, and to him the vehicle is only sacred when the deceased is in it. Steve was hungry, the boys were hungry, and he was going to get something to eat. They pulled round the back of McDonald's, got out of the hearse and had a feast. The boys, pretty young at the time, were shocked, knowing that this would never happen with me, but they enjoyed the food anyway. Although we do things very differently and carry out a completely different kind of work in the funeral industry, Steve is trustworthy and honest. The people he serves would have no problem with his stopping off for a Big Mac, and he would tell them, 'Listen, it's not just the hearse that wanted filling, it's me as well!' A kind and devout man; a real star.

The closest we have ever come to McDonald's on a funeral occurred in 2003, when we were returning from a crematorium with the family. Simon was driving the first limousine, in which were seven members of the family, one sitting in the front with him. So, naturally, I was in the front of the second car, following him back to the family address, which on this occasion was a social club where there was to be plenty of food and drink for all. The funeral had been huge – about nine cars and several hundred members of the family and friends attending. We had also been into church, and the funeral was already into its fourth hour.

As we drove round by the World of Leather roundabout at Eltham and down towards the Yorkshire Grey roundabout, I could see a sign: 'McDonald's drive-in. Twenty chicken nuggets special £2.99.' I could also see lots of activity in the back of Simon's car. Lots of hands pointing out of the windows, lots of looking round at me. I guessed what was going on.

'Simon, Simon,' the man in the front had said, 'Mother loved a chicken nugget. In here, boy, into the left. We'll get chicken nuggets all around – £2.99, what a bargain!'

Caught off balance for a second, Simon headed the car to the left, not knowing quite whether or not the family were serious. Then his professionalism took him over and he glided directly past, everyone in the car laughing. He simply said, 'If I pull in there, I am dead. My dad will kill me.' He was not wrong; I taught him well. How everybody laughed.

As we pulled up at the social club, I got out, looked at Simon and said in front of everybody, 'Well done, son, I'm proud of you. In McDonald's – well I never!'

'Oh, you said your dad would say that. We were trying to get him to go in. Mum loved a chicken nugget. Cor blimey, Barry, we could have had a big box of chicken nuggets each.'

'Come on,' I said to them all, 'you know me better than that.'

'Ah yes. He said you wouldn't have that.'

Then, to my total amazement, because we were at that time on the television every week they all insisted on autographs. I had to sign the back of all the service sheets so that they could hand them out to their family to show who did the funeral. You cannot get nicer people than that. I was embarrassed by their generosity and kindness, and Simon did brilliantly – a chip off the old block. He loves chicken nuggets, so this was a big sacrifice to true professionalism.

Another funny moment came as we were leaving a Catholic church after taking a deceased person in on the evening before the service. We turned left on to Jamaica Road, into the first part of the bus lane so that we could get along and into the outer lane of the roundabout. As we did, we were passed by two girls in a car. When they saw us, they started to shout across through their open window: "Ere, get out of the bus lane; queue like the rest of us!' It was Penny and Sarah, two local girls who do catering and whose husbands I know very well.

'Mind your own business,' I said. 'Get on with your catering. What do you know?' We were of course all laughing.

But Penny had stopped concentrating on the road, and I started trying to bring her attention to what was ahead. The car in front of her had stopped – but she did not. Bang. Directly into it.

'See,' I said. 'Mind your own business and pay attention to the road.'

Luckily there was no damage to either her car or the one in front. It just shows how endearing the people of Bermondsey can be and how well we all know each other. Just like the Bible says, 'There is a time for everything: a time to laugh and a time to cry.' I had both those at once then.

Not everything is so humorous in our profession, though. On a more serious note, there have been so many changes in recent years in our industry. Health and safety has of course come very much to the fore in how we prepare our embalming rooms, our vehicles and our lifting equipment, and in how our staff are monitored and cared for. We have an air cushion that will take a weight of up to 75 stone and lift a deceased person up to trolley height with dignity. Disabled facilities, purpose-built vehicles, awareness and of course comfortable and luxurious funeral homes where funerals can be arranged and the dead may lie in peace have become necessities. What has not changed, of course, and is central to our work, is the care of the deceased and the bereaved, and our attention to detail in these matters.

The funerals of children and the bereavement care of their families have always held a special place in my life as a funeral director. I was fortunate to be involved in the setting up of bereavement care related to foetuses, stillborn infants and children who die at Guy's Hospital. I have been invited to give lectures to midwives, and occasionally nurses and midwives visit the funeral home trying to understand better what goes on after the child leaves the hospital and how a funeral is planned and arranged. I have made sure there is a special plot for children at our local cemetery and that the crematorium is well organised and prepared for the cremation of children. More recently, I have been able to help prepare an information booklet, working with Molly, a superb midwife carer at St Thomas' Hospital and a lady whom I greatly admire.

It has been recently decided that mothers who lose a child may, if they wish, carry the baby from the hospital themselves in their arms or in a carry cot and take the baby home for several days, thereby giving them time to separate and give back their child for burial or cremation. Although this can be quite lovely in itself, there are many hidden difficulties. How can we monitor that the parents have actually gone ahead with a funeral? Or that the house is suitable for the baby to be left in at that time? Or that the parents will be able to cope with that difficulty? Do they have enough support and help? I have made myself and Albin's available as a funeral company to give that sort of support to the hospital, and advice when it is asked for. It is very important to help a family to take part in any segment of the funeral, or the whole funeral, or just to give guidance and assistance so that people feel they personally have some control at that level. Today, we are willing to listen to whatever people want to do and, within reason, try to achieve it for them.

However, about a year ago, when the hospital first started this scheme, we had no knowledge that it was in place or that such a scheme could be set up. A lady just simply walked into our reception with a little baby who had died in her arms – not that you could honestly tell, as it just looked as if the baby was asleep. She gave the baby to Jackie and said, 'This is my baby. I've just brought her straight from the hospital, and I would like you to bury her please, quietly, some time in the next week or so, and let me know when so that I can come along.'

Jackie got the mother to sit down and gave her some tea. We phoned the hospital because we had had no experience in this area and we wanted to be sure that the lady had not just walked out of the hospital without anybody's knowledge. Sure enough, the hospital explained that it was a new procedure and admitted that we should have been contacted and some agreement set up between us. That is when Molly came in: 'Barry,' she said, 'we need to meet. I think it would be a really good idea if we made an information booklet for families who want to do this kind of thing.'

This we did, and now I feel more comfortable that there are at least safety and follow-up procedures in place so that such a kindness to a family can provide help and not become a disaster.

We have a little baby section in our Memorial Garden, and it is quite beautiful. On a small lawn, bricked all around the edge, stands a little cherub. Families can have their babies' ashes scattered here, and little markers bearing the babies' names go into the grass. When we extend our garden in 2005, I greatly hope to have a much bigger section that will encompass foetuses and stillborn babies and provide a private walled area where families can gather from time to time. A place to go, really. This is, I believe, very important.

Our Memorial Garden Cremation Cemetery, as we call it, has been a wonderful success. It has now been open for about four years, with over two thousand sets of ashes and families now connected to it. Over three thousand people attended our last annual Memorial Garden service, on a cold December evening, a very special service that has now become legendary in the area. We had some beautiful carols. Two fantastic professional classical singers performed 'Somewhere Over the Rainbow' and 'You'll Never Walk Alone', and our very own Father Alan sang the more modern 'Softly as I Leave You', which was beautifully appropriate. We released twelve doves and produced some beautiful music for the evening, as well as some lovely readings of the liturgy, and readings about kindness and bereavement, delivered by some eight ministers of different religions. My two sons also read, as did Jon Fletcher and Joanna. We finished with a beautiful firework exploding into the sky towards the stars with all our best wishes and love, and a wonderful sign that lit up as a firework saying 'Peace' in lilac and blue, all perfectly scripted to music.

People were also able to take a flower and lay it, as they left the garden, as a final remembrance at our special crib, which we had built for the occasion. Finally, everybody was invited to mince pies, soup and mulled wine, tea and coffee. Amazingly, like the biblical feeding of the five thousand, it somehow all went round, and those who stayed were there for almost an hour afterwards, not wanting the moment to end. Through a friend, we were able to produce an amateur video and make it available to the local community.

Every year, we choose a charity to support and do everything we can as a firm to help it in every way. For 2004, this has been the Evelina Children's Hospital, for which I am a trustee of the committee that needs to collect some £10 million to make the hospital the most special children's hospital there could ever be. And, I can tell you, every one of us is determined to see that happen.

The Evelina Children's Hospital has been a very famous hospital over the years in Southwark. It is where I spent the first few days of my life as a child and also where I had my tonsils removed, where I was for some time having suffered with whooping cough and where I recovered from another delicate 'boy's' operation that I'd sooner forget! However, I have a lot to thank that hospital for, and the wonderful staff who have worked there over the years. So many people in the Bermondsey area have benefited from the Evelina. It is only right that they and many others – including big businesses – should contribute to making it the finest place for children to be treated in the future.

The Evelina Trust recently ran a function at Buckingham Palace, with many wealthy bankers and successful business-men attending. It was indeed a great honour for me to attend and to be one of the only eight people presented to Her Royal Highness Princess Anne that evening. I was introduced by Stanley Fink, the head of a financial company in the City, as Southwark's local representative on the Trust committee. Princess Anne was very charming and asked me what local work we were doing. When I said how I had spent the first days of my life in that particular hospital, she humorously retorted, 'Oh, you have been on the committee a long time, then. I didn't think we would be going back that far.'

The evening was a great success and raised a lot of money for the hospital. For Jackie and myself, it was a very memorable evening and a great honour. The committee had been able to raise some £2½ million out of the £10 million that is required. Although this seems a huge amount, I have a feeling that, one way or another, we will get there as a team. The main children's building will of course be built by the NHS, on the site of St Thomas' Hospital; the £10 million that we are attempting to raise will enable the hospital to have the smartest of rooms. Beds that pull out alongside the child's bed or cot so that a parent can stay. Lovely gardens for the children to be in when they are recovering. A special babies' room, computer rooms, long-stay rooms, a school, special scanners – the icing on the cake.

The local Bermondsey people have taken this charity to their hearts, and we get regular phone calls asking us to collect big bunny rabbits or teddy bears – all donated by local people – for raffling or to be placed in the babies' rooms in the hospital. The bowls club in Southwark Park arranged a fantastic day in July 2004 for a bowls tournament and a fun day. They asked Albin's to put forward a team of nine and play the police, the Southwark Park Club, the nurses, etc., all to raise money for the Evelina Hospital. They said we could turn up in black, but no top hats please, and there were three golden rules to abide by: 1 No burials on the greens; 2 No ashes scattered on the greens; 3 No memorials put on the greens. In other words, they don't mind us digging in, but they don't want us digging down!

Millwall Football Club, our local 2004 FA Cup semi-finalists, have also held a collection day. They are very community conscious and a great support. Unfortunately, negative comments are all too often – and all too often unfairly – heard about Millwall, the positive side being overlooked.

Up the Lions
We are very proud of you round here!

11

MY LIFE (AND MORE) IN A FLASH

Many people comment that frames of your life flash in front of your eyes moments before your death. Well, I do not know whether or not that is true, but as we approach the end of our lives we often look back on what might have been. Could we have done things differently? Do we have any regrets? How wonderful it would be not to have any regrets. But whatever we might say to those close to us, I truly doubt that there is anyone who has never had a regret, or who would not have done things differently, in some small way at least.

I for one have spent my lifetime serving people, but that honestly does not mean that I am their servant. Being a funeral director has been a great privilege – and knowing what I know now, I do not think I would change that – but it has brought with it great obligations, obligations that, even in my private life, on holiday and during sleep, never leave me. I have often wondered how relieved I might be without those obligations and, then again, how empty that would leave me.

I carry the historical mantle of the generations who have gone before me in this profession and through Albin's. What I often think will be wonderful in the future is that my sons will have each other to share that burden and, thank God, through each other might achieve some peace of mind. The one honest thing I can say is that I do not have genuine peace of mind. There are many reasons for this, and in some ways I am my own worst enemy as I take the full responsibility of death and the task of caring for the bereaved to heart.

Of course, there are other people with great responsibilities in life: teachers, doctors, lawyers, drivers, pilots . . . I could go on and on and on. Whatever our careers, we all have obligations and responsibilities to others, and I do not belittle any other profession by my statement. One's occupation, however humble, is without doubt a true honour. It does not matter whether you serve burgers, sweep streets or look after the sick, everybody has an important role to play in life. But the responsibility and often the burden of carrying the sacredness of death without any dress rehearsal is a grave responsibility in every way.

There is something unique about being a funeral director that is not explainable in words. It is a feeling of holding the key to a sacred or secret door that you must be there to open. 'The dead never leave you'; I constantly remind people of that. They are a tremendous force of energy that surrounds us. Their physical absence brings us pain, but the force they leave supports us and helps us to fight life's battles. Often that is what life is like, a constant battle that we fight, yet when it ends we can perhaps look back and see how unimportant were the small things that upset us. I hope I am making sense, and I hope that my words will allow us all to gain a little strength to cope better with loss, and allow us to enjoy the time we have left without regret. Now that would be time worth having. In the big circle of life, we are all just the spokes of a wheel: remove one spoke and the wheel's strength is reduced, remove several spokes and the wheel could easily collapse. In this way, in our existence alone we make a difference.

I have said often that, on my deathbed, I would like to say, 'One minute more, please.' It is human nature to want to extend your life and hang on to every last moment. I often think about being on my deathbed, hopefully with a priest standing next to me giving me my last rites (but not Father Alan, though – I have every intention of outliving him!). I sometimes picture that last moment in my mind and think how I would feel.

The priest would be saying, 'May Christ welcome you and drive away the Devil.' I think I would have to stop him there:

'Hang on a minute, Father; this is not the time for me to be making any enemies, especially of the Devil.'

Well, you have got to have every base covered, haven't you? I would not like to die or leave this world without a little humour, and one thing is certain, I do not want to leave this world owing anyone any money. I want all my debts paid, the slate wiped clean.

A number of years ago I was involved in a sporting business venture. In fact, we were directors of a football club. Anybody who has been a director of a football club will know that you constantly have to put your hand in your pocket to keep it running. Football clubs in general are bottomless pits, and in my experience there is no money to be made from such ventures – you just have to love the game. On the board with me were a number of Bermondsey people, real characters, and a number of other directors from different parts of London and from different cultures. As always, the Bermondsey boys came up with the money first when asked, and it was honestly always a struggle to get the money from the North London guys (not that I have anything against North London, but for me it's just not Bermondsey, is it?).

This one particular guy was a really nice person but was always saying he was hard up or skint. We never really believed him, but he would always be the last one to put his money in – if at all. When he sadly died a number of years ago, it came to light that he left an estate amounting to quite a few million pounds. When one of my fellow ex-directors found this out, he popped into the office and said to me, ''Ere, Bal, you 'eard 'ow much stuff Staffos left?'

'I have, Terry.'

'Well, that's what I have come in to see you about, Bal.'

'What do you want me to do, Terry?' I asked him.

'I want you to dig him up, Bal.'

'Dig him up?' I queried.

'Yeah, so I can get him by the throat and call him a bloody liar. All the times he didn't put in and he has left all that money. The lousy git' (forgive my language here).

You see, you can't beat a Bermondsey sense of humour. Although I am sure Terry would tell me he was not joking, I know he was, and there is certainly no malice intended, he was just telling it the way it was. For me, harm and stupidity would be saying to someone whose name was Mohammed, 'That must be a very common Christian name', as somebody I once knew did! For me, this was just Terry's way of coping with the financial shock.

When you are a funeral director, you hear so many stories, most of them amusing; after all, there is no other profession in the world that could have an accident involving four of its vehicles in which no one at all was hurt yet there were four dead at the scene. It could only happen to a funeral director (well, one with four hearses, of course).

It is no good crying about what might have been in this life: you just have to get on with the cards you are dealt. And it is no good being vengeful or bitter when the cards are not dealt in your favour because that would destroy every last moment you have left in this life. Make the best of a bad lot. As the song says, 'Always look on the bright side of life', a very poignant message for us all.

The Italian funeral director I know in New York – the lady I met on holiday in the last chapter – relayed to me one brilliant example of somebody who made the very best of a bad situation when she was given a rather unfortunate opportunity. This particular lady had lost her husband, a gentleman who had lived quite a frugal life, never being overgenerous and always claiming he never had anything left financially for the little pleasures in life. When he died, his ever-faithful and loyal wife arranged, with my Italian funeral director friend, a beautiful funeral with a lovely Italian casket. She knew she was getting herself into debt with this but she wanted to give her poor husband the best because he had in truth – or so she thought – never been able to afford the best in life. One of the husband's last wishes, clearly indicated in his will, was for him to be buried with a special picture that he had kept since his wedding day of his wife in her beautiful white wedding dress. How touching, you may think.

The picture which the wife thought was the precious possession her husband wanted to take with him to the grave was mounted in a beautiful frame. The funeral director, after discussing it with the wife, suggested that she should keep the frame as a memento as it was so beautiful and old. She agreed, saying that she would put a copy of the photo back in it to keep with her and remember her dear husband by. What a devoted husband he seemed, and how moved the wife was by his gesture to be buried with her picture.

But as the funeral director removed the photo from the frame, she found, hidden in the back, $50,000 in large bills, which of course she immediately returned to the widow. She was shocked rigid and, in a raging temper, changed the whole funeral to a basic cremation, calling her husband a lying, cheating pig (ouch). The moral of this true story is that this lady spent every penny of that $50,000 enjoying the remainder of the time she had left in this world. The man, of course, was unsuccessful not only in taking the money with him but also in getting his final wish to be buried. He was cremated and scattered to the winds – that was his final fate. How sad is that?

Italian funerals have always interested me, particularly the beautiful coffins they use. My curiosity has led me to spend some lovely moments in Italy around Lake Garda and our coffin factory, owned by the Ferrari family (not the car manufacturer, unfortunately!). On one of my purchasing visits there, I heard a radio advertisement calling for people to come and cry at a funeral, an old Italian tradition I am told. Looking through the old National Association of Funeral Directors (NAFD) journals from 1958, I came across the following small but interesting article relating an old memory of some very strange Italian funeral practices:

6 March 1958 . . . It is almost worth dying in Italy – just for the sake of the funeral. First of all you are put into a beautiful coffin; this is only on loan and is returned to the carpenter when you finally disappear. The coffin is

put into a glass hearse adorned with brass angels and copper cherubs, and is drawn by four black horses, which in turn are preceded by a long procession of Methuselahs [Methuselah being the 'old man' of the Bible, who reputedly lived to 969 years old] and very young children draped in white sheets and red waistcoats. They take no interest in the funeral, but walk in front to clear the way. Behind the hearse, the village band plays a dirge and is followed by the relatives and the officiating priests. But the best part comes when the funeral is over. For some reason there is a great rush by the professional supporters to get back. The other day I met one of these funerals returning; I couldn't get out of the way quick enough. In a cloud of dust, the hearse, minus the body, came careering down the road. Inside the glass case sat the older Methuselahs, while outside were the children screaming and shouting, clinging for dear life to the brass angels, their robes flowing in the wind. Sitting on the horses, the two trumpeters from the band were blowing something like a post-horn gallop, and the steeds responded accordingly. One hour later, the same procession appeared in all its sombre glory, but this time there was a different body in the hearse.

Certainly not an Albin funeral that one – far too hurried!

Funeral customs never fail to amaze me but always intrigue me. A more recent statement in the NAFD magazine entitled 'Mummy appeal':

A television company are producing a documentary on the ancient Egyptian process of mummification. With the help of British Museum Egyptologist Dr Joyce Filer and pathologists, we will recreate a genuine Egyptian burial, employing actual mummification procedures and ancient burial rites.

This will be a landmark documentary, to be accompanied by a book, and will be made with utmost sensitivity to the individual and family involved. The documentary will be historical and educational, and not sensational.

To that end, we are seeking a recently deceased corpse, which has been donated specifically for this purpose. I would be most grateful to hear from any Funeral Director who gets a request for this type of burial. I can be reached at -- TV. Thank you very much.

Producer

Any takers? If you have read my last book, *Final Departures*, you may remember Mr Iouannou - the gentleman who mummified his mummy. This would have been right up his street, I think, and all for free, too. To this day, however, I do not know that anybody has actually taken up this offer. I have never heard any more about it, although the producer concerned did contact me to see whether I had undertaken such a procedure. I of course referred her to the chapter called 'Embalmondsey' in *Final Departures*, but I never heard any more from her, and I would not anyway take part in such a venture. An interesting project, but I would be surprised if the programme is ever made. Mind you, stranger things have happened, you just never know.

You think you have heard it all, but you never have. If, like me, you are a connoisseur of the unusual, you are always looking openly to the extraordinary, which then often presents itself when you have the imagination to look for it in the first place. I hope from this chapter that, if nothing else, you get my point that life and death go hand in hand. They are inseparable and rarely ordinary in their presentation. We live in a remarkable world and incredible times, and I feel that I work in the most amazing of professions, saturated with experiences that have truly enriched my life, even if the only colour in my spectrum is black. For all this, my life is, and has been, no less colourful. On the contrary, it has been a rainbow of experiences – good, bad, happy and sad. Full of so many emotions but rarely ordinary because we are all human and honestly know so little. Maybe that is why faith is so immeasurable and important, certainly to me anyway.

I read in a magazine once that you can talk to your parents about anything. (Oh yeah, is this train of thought for real?) This is a great concept and it must be a genuine gift for those few people for whom it is possible. In reality, though, I believe it to be rarely achievable. There are some things that we should never share with a parent, private and personal things that they would not want to share with us anyway. On the other hand, children's positive perception of a parent is vital to the existence of a proud family unit.

What I do believe to be honestly essential in this life as a parent or a child is to express our feelings to one another while we have the chance. How often have you heard it said, and quite rightly too, 'It's too late when we die.' Don't leave it so late that you have the opportunity taken from you, leaving you full of regret and with the emptiness of a lost moment, when what could have been said is left unsaid. It is a well-known psychological fact that people respond badly to commands, so I will not order you here, or even try the art of gentle persuasion, but let this be a wake-up call from somebody who knows: don't put off until tomorrow what you can do today. If you truly need to tell somebody how much you love them, clear your mind or get something off your chest off, do it. Then you will have no regrets and your moment will not be taken from you. This is so vitally important. Put this book down and go and tell the closest people in your life just how you feel. If you are really lucky, this moment may change your life and in the fullness of time leave you complete, warm and full rather than empty. Reconciliation can be a wonderful healer of the soul.

Every living human being has a gift, but sometimes we do not know what it is. Sometimes we do not know how to find it or even where to begin. Yet I believe it is actually really simple, the real trick lying not in the search for the ability but in its channelling. We may only need a little jolt and our gift will flow like a fountain for all to see. For some of us, though, an atomic explosion is needed to ignite the power within, so it remains hidden and is never perceived as a talent. For those who never find their fuse, they may feel, at the end of their life, more than just a little regret, perhaps even anger, at what could have been. Even those of us who need an atom bomb to start us off should search and strive to find our purpose in this life, however humble it may seem. There is hope for everyone. What I am persistently trying to say here in so many ways is: grasp the moment, don't let it pass you by; don't wait for the dreaded words, 'It's too late.'

My own mum died when I was seventeen, and I lamented, and still do, that I did not get the chance to say goodbye. When I really think about it, though, that is all I did not get the chance to do, because every day I told her I loved her and she did the same, so we were both secure in that knowledge. I still miss her terribly some thirty-six years after her death. She is a force that will always be with me, and I would of course love her to be here to see my achievements, my life, her grandchildren and great-grandchildren, and to be with her whole family again. I know that cannot be, but I truly believe that she is aware of all these beautiful things. She is with me in my most difficult times and my greatest achievements. I see her often in myself and my children, and sometimes in the smiles of my grandchildren. In so many ways, she still exists. For me, it would be ridiculous to believe that all ended here – her existence was too powerful for that. We have to let go, but we do not have to forget; in fact; I don't think we ever can.

When we lose someone, our life changes and, in a way, a little of ourselves dies with them. The funeral is the first step, the first move, towards acceptance and genuine healing. We cannot repair our bodies if we cannot repair our minds. We must take those first early steps when we experience loss, even though they seem of little importance at the time because we are numb and unable to perceive what is going on around us. However, we eventually come to understand how necessary they were. If we do not see that, those first steps were never correctly taken and at that point we honestly need help. Do not underestimate bereavement and loss: it is an evil illness if left untreated.

People often ask me what I would have been if I hadn't been a funeral director, but for me that is like saying I would not exist because I would not have been me. I cannot really think of myself as anything else. Being a funeral director has been a part of my whole life from birth – it was not something I just started doing when I was twenty, after my education. It is something I believe I was born to do. Yes, of course I wanted to do all the boyish things like being a footballer or a policeman or a doctor, and I am sure they all would have been really interesting professions. I enjoyed my schooling and sport, and I know I am the greatest footballer never to have been capped, but that's in my dreams. And that is what is wonderful about dreams: we can live our realities through them. But, in a way, I was never really given a choice. Today, that might well be frowned upon, but I see it differently. If I can't be what I am, I don't want to be anything else, and being a funeral director is what I am. As a result, I have been able to incorporate so much else into my existence.

Being a funeral director has enabled me to see so much of life. I have been able to become a magistrate, businessman, bereavement counsellor, poor man's lawyer and Dickensian Friend. I have been involved in education as a school governor, and I have been a charitable trustee. Most of all, being a funeral director has enabled me to make a difference – who could ask for more? So if I couldn't be a funeral director, what would I be? – lost I think! I could always be an undertaker, I suppose – oh no, that's the same thing, isn't it? By any other name, what I do is what I do.

The boys and I sometimes manage to carve out a moment in the day to go and see something we are thinking of buying. We will often be in our work clothes and one of the boys might say to me, 'Oh Dad, can't I get changed before I go?' But I always say to them, 'You must never be ashamed of your work clothes. On the contrary, be proud of them.'

They are good boys and take my point, but I cannot really blame them for preferring their designer gear. One thing I promise you though, boys, if I manage to get old I will try not to be a silly old fool, honest I will. After all, I probably drive you mad now; what I would be like if I became a silly old fool? It would not be worth thinking about. Joking aside, my message in this chapter is that life is just too short. If there is one thing that being a funeral director has taught me, it is to experience every moment and not miss a second. Death comes too quickly.

> I have felt your pain
> I have seen your despair
> It's a symbol of your love for me, and how you care
>
> 'WHY DID YOU LEAVE?'
> I heard you say
> I had to, that's God's way.
>
> You're expected to grieve the loss of me,
> For loss at this moment is all that you see
> Recognise me as the sunlight
>
> Hear me during the storm
> See my shadow through the rain
> As you feel the pain . . . refrain . . .
> And let it go.
>
> I've lived life's experiences
> Its joys and its fears,
> Felt the grievances and sometimes the tears . . .
> There is no answer as to why things happen the way
> that they do
>
> But look into your heart
> I'll always be there
> I'll always be with you.
>
> You need never walk alone.

Written for our 2003 memorial service
by our son Jonathan

12

BACK TO THE FUTURE

The truth is sometimes stranger than life itself, and having read through this book you may well be thinking what an accurate statement that is. I never fail to be amazed by my life and the experiences it confronts me with daily as a funeral director.

I recently visited Dublin on a business trip to meet the Fanagan brothers, who run Wm Fanagan, a lovely old traditional firm of family funeral directors. We took a cab from the airport to Fanagan's, an uneventful journey and not too expensive, I thought. The cab itself, however, seemed to be a simple car, not easily recognisable as a taxi cab. Later that evening, when I was having dinner with the Fanagans, I asked them whether there was any regulation on becoming a taxi driver. One of the Fanagan boys laughed and said to me, 'You know cabs in Dublin are about to accept credit cards as well as cash? When you do pay by card, you will have to show two forms of ID.'

'Well, that sounds reasonable,' I replied.

'To be sure it is, but that's two more than you need to become a Dublin cab driver.'

'Fair enough,' I said. 'So it's not really regulated?'

'Not so you would notice.'

And he went on to tell me a true story about a guy who had recently became a cab driver. The driver was driving along with a passenger in the back. It was a fairly steady ride, and the driver was in a bit of a trance, when suddenly the passenger tapped the driver on the shoulder to ask him something. The driver let out a yell, made a crucial mistake and pulled the car over on to the pavement, just missing a post and stopping only feet from a shop window. For a moment, both the passenger and the driver were completely silent in shock.

Then the driver said suddenly, 'Please don't ever do that again; you scared the living daylights out of me.'

The passenger, completely shaken by this time, apologised and said that he did not realise that a tap on the shoulder would have such an effect.

The driver replied, 'Look, I am sorry, it's me who should be apologising, it's not your fault at all. This is my first day driving this cab, and I have got to tell you I have been driving a hearse for the last twenty-five years, and psychologically I was miles away driving my hearse. The tap on the shoulder you gave me was one that I have dreaded for the last twenty-five years.'

Well, it would give you a jolt, wouldn't it, when you have driven a hearse for so long. That can be a lonely job, and one in which sudden company could give you a bit of a shock.

I was not sure whether this was a bit of Fanagan blarney, but when I was looking through the *Irish Post* at the airport, there in Column HQ was the same story – it had happened only a few days before. I smiled to myself as I imagined the shock it must have been for both the cab driver and the passenger. A nice Irish member of our church has also recently given me a cutting of this story – great!

About a month ago, we had the funeral of a local lady, her lovely family visiting her daily where she was lying in our chapel. Every single day, they would arrive at about midday and stay until around six o'clock in the evening, talking to their mum in the chapel and having the odd cup of tea with us, making the most of the time they had left with Mum. They were terrific people and made themselves completely at home with us, something I really like to see. As you walked past them in reception, they would say hello, chat or ask what was going on. Amazingly, though, having their mum there led to some very strange happenings.

Now, all the lighting and electrical circuits in our building are really only a year or so old. They have all been renewed and are in excellent working order, yet when the family arrived every day – and I do mean when they arrived – three lights at the end of the corridor outside the chapel would suddenly go off. As the family went to and fro between the chapel where Mum was lying and our reception area, the lights would continue to go on or off. On one occasion, the girls stopped me and said, ''Ere Bal, see what our mum's doing. She's turning your lights on and off just to let us know she is here.'

I smiled, not really believing that this had anything to do with their mum but thinking that there was nothing wrong with them feeling that way. Just as they were telling me this, I turned my head to where they had pointed and, quite unbelievably, the lights went off completely.

''Ere you are, told you, Barry,' they said. 'Look, Mum's turned them off just to show you.'

'Well, there must be a loose light,' I replied.

'No,' they said, 'I bet there's not. I bet it's our mum.'

I turned around again and the lights came back on. 'See, she's making sure you know.'

I smiled with them, still not completely convinced. At that point, about six o'clock, the family left, so I walked straight down the corridor to the three lights, set in a panel. I tapped around the panel and the lights themselves – nothing. There was no vibration, shaking or movement. They were quite firm. No loose bulbs. As I turned around, I saw the family looking through the window at me, laughing because I was testing the lights.

I walked outside to them and said, 'Do you know, there's no loose connection there. They seem to be fine.'

'It's our mum, Barry,' the daughter said. 'It's our mum, honest.'

As God is my witness, this happened every day for the ten days they visited and stopped when they left. And from the day of their mother's funeral, when she left our chapel, I have not experienced a single problem with those lights. Our electrician Gary, an old school friend, has checked them out too, and there appears to be no problem whatsoever. Having seen that family every day for ten days, I have to say I quite miss them. You get very attached to people in this job, especially people like them. I guess their mum left us that day too, not just in body, but also in spirit.

We sometimes push away the pain so much that we disconnect from ourselves and often from the truth. Never is that seen to be truer than when dealing with bereavement. I was conducting the funeral of a lady who had died in Casualty of a heart attack. After the funeral, I stayed with the family in the garden looking at the flowers and collecting the cards for them. It was a small funeral, and the husband, an elderly and very kindly gentleman, asked to sit in the front with me on the return journey.

As we undertook the short journey back from the crematorium, he looked across at me and said, 'You know, it's the strangest thing, but I felt so silly at the hospital.'

'You mustn't feel like that,' I replied.

'No,' he said, 'what happened was that my wife came over quite bad at home and I thought to myself, she's having a heart attack. I thought, I'm not going to ring for an ambulance, you don't know how long that might take. I got her straight in the car, as it is only a short journey to the hospital, and I drove straight up to Casualty. I ran in and got somebody to come out with a chair to help her, put her in the chair and they took her in. I went and parked the car, came back in and asked where my wife was. They said, she's being treated in the room just along the corridor and would I kindly wait just outside the door. There was a lot of activity, and I didn't know what was going on.

'After a while, a doctor came out and sat down next to me. He said, "Mr Roberts, I am sorry to have to tell you that your wife has gone."

' "Gone, what do you mean gone? I've got the car, she can't have gone."

' "No," he said, "Mr Roberts, I am sorry, I mean that your wife has passed away, she has died."

'I felt such a fool. She couldn't have got the car, what was I thinking of? You've got to laugh, haven't you? What a silly old sod I was. I didn't know what he was talking about. I didn't think for a minute she was going to die, honest I didn't.'

I told Mr Roberts I thought he acted so naturally and that there was nothing wrong with what he said. Looking back, of course, it sounds funny, and Mr Roberts can see the funny side of it himself now too. But I guess that, at the time, he was just disconnecting and pushing away the truth. Experiencing denial. Or maybe, even simpler than that, he just got hold of the wrong end of the stick. From time to time, Mr Roberts visits the little rose tree he has for his wife, and I will never forget our drive back from the crematorium.

Being a funeral director has taught me not to assume anything but to check the truth carefully. It has also taught me to think about what I say and not just say what is in my mind. Should we speak our minds irrespective of what it does to somebody or whom it hurts? Should we just tell it how it is, no matter what? No, we shouldn't. Suspicion and speculation can be pointless and often unkind. Only firm evidence and proof are the roads to the ability and the right to tell it as it is. Any other way is truly destructive, painful and clearly unfair. Yet even with firm evidence, one should be thoughtful and not reckless. We should always remember that, whatever the circumstances, there are always other people to be considered.

Yes, it is ultimately always better to tell the truth even if it hurts, but sometimes, through the milk of human kindness, we can tell the truth conservatively and in small doses, for example using the words 'passed away' instead of simply 'died'. We do this, of course, to cushion the pain that the truth can bring, which is exactly what the doctor was trying to do when he told poor old Mr Roberts that his wife had 'gone'. He could not bring himself to say that Mrs Roberts had died. Perhaps it would have been better if he had. But, then again, the story has left Mr Roberts with a pleasant memory of that moment, or at least a kind one, and, with time, he is now able to look back and smile more often than he cries. There is something nice about that, isn't there? We are all different – that's what makes life so special and death even more complicated.

In Southwark Park Road, deep in the heart of Bermondsey, is a place we call 'the Blue' where there is a little marketplace of stalls. Florrie Weller, the flower lady, is somebody straight out of *Mary Poppins*, a beautiful old character who has run her family stall with her son for longer than I can recall. I often buy plants from her and stop for a chat; whenever I walk a funeral through the Blue, I always stop and tip my hat to her, and she politely acknowledges.

We were chatting away the other week when she reminded me of a funeral that Fred Albin had conducted when I was a lad, a real old costermonger funeral with plenty of cars and plenty of flowers. I remember the funeral because I was a bearer at the time and not yet driving. Everybody in the family was in attendance. Two of the in-laws, young sons-in-law I think, agreed to stay behind and prepare a proper Bermondsey spread of sandwiches, sausage rolls, jellied eels and all the trimmings. I remember it was a very windy day, and Fred had taken particular care to tie the flowers down carefully so as not to lose any. Florrie recalled the whole event with amazing clarity, bringing the whole scene back to me.

At the graveside at the end of the service, one of the mourners' hats blew down into the grave. Having paid quite a lot of money for the hat, he insisted on getting it back so the poor grave-digger had to clamber down the side of the grave, without stepping on the coffin, to retrieve it. The mourner gave him half a crown for that – nice money if you can get it, some might think, but not a very pleasant thing to have to do. When you are inside a grave, it's not much fun looking up, I promise you.

We then made our way back to the house only to find that both boys had been on the beer and were fast asleep in the chairs. Not a sandwich cut, not a jellied eel prepared, not a sausage roll cooked. Nothing to eat. And in Bermondsey, we are hospitable people so feeding the mourners after a funeral is essential. There was hell to pay – no food, and a lot of the booze had gone. The girls of course rolled up their sleeves to prepare the food, the lads had a whip-round for some extra beer, and within an hour or so everyone was being fed and watered.

Florrie recalled that her main concern was not being able to give Fred and the boys a sandwich, which she considered to be very embarrassing, but she remembers that Fred popped back in the evening to have a drink with them, something he often did anyway! He was such a kind and good funeral director. He and Florrie had also gone to school together and are still good friends today. As for Florrie, she is the salt of the earth, and the Blue would not be the same place without her. Long may she reign!

So there we are. I am now fifty-three years of age and, I would say, at the prime of my life as a funeral director. It is my moment, my time, and I hope there is much more to come, perhaps even a third *Don't Drop the Coffin* to take me to my own *Final Departure*. If nothing else, I will always expect the unexpected and will of course hang on to my moment for as long as I can. Indeed, one of my proudest moments has come just as I finish writing this book – I have just been elected President of FIAT-IFTA, the international association of funeral directors.

The real skill will, I think, lie in knowing when my moment has passed and when it is best to hand the mantle over to those whose moment is yet to come – my two sons Simon and

Jonathan. I certainly hope that I have that wisdom and courage, the two qualities I feel are most needed to go through such a transition. If you stay in control and in charge for too long, you can do more harm than good. It would be lovely to stay on and help the boys in their work when they need me – not when I think they need me but when *they* ask. I have said all this many times before, which at least shows that I am very aware of it and conscious that it is something I will eventually have to do. Like anyone else, I have had both good and bad fortune in my life, but overall it has been fairly balanced and rewarding. As I said in the previous chapter, I think there is little I would change because regret is too painful an intention and will make one's memories and dreams unhappy.

If I could have changed anything physically, I would have chosen better eyesight. I did not like wearing glasses as a teenager so I often left them off, even though I needed them. Playing football would certainly have been even more fun if I could have seen who I was playing with from week to week! I was about twenty-nine before I got contact lenses, and it was only then that I realised how much I had been missing. In my football, I had never been very good in the air, and I honestly thought contact lenses would much improve the situation. Unfortunately, once I got them I realised that I close my eyes when I head the ball anyway, so it would have made very little difference over the years.

There have, however, been occasions when it would have been nice to have seen a little more. I often go to the gym with my sons, and our chauffeur Lee often comes with us. One evening, Lee and I were sitting in the jacuzzi chatting away, as you do, when, to Lee's disbelief, two stunning and hugely endowed blondes in bikinis got into the jacuzzi with us. They were, it turned out, 'page three girls' who had been photographed at the gym earlier and had now decided to relax in the jacuzzi. Lee could not believe his luck. Lee being Lee, of course, he decided to chat to them, enjoying every moment. Sadly, without my glasses, I could see very little – just the outline shapes – so I was unable to appreciate my extraordinary opportunity. I really would have benefited from better eyesight that evening, but then again I am grateful to have my eyesight, however bad it is. Luckily, every cloud has a silver lining, and Lee gleefully filled me in on the details. Of course, being a gentleman, I would have averted my eyes anyway . . . I don't think!

So, assuming at this point in my life that Albin's and I are inseparable, where are we both now in the world of funeral directing? Throughout its history, Albin's has been blessed with good leaders, and I hope that in the fullness of time I might be seen as one of them. Historically, we always seem to have made good decisions, and the present time is definitely no exception. My sons and I now have the business exactly where we would like it to be. Not so small as to be uneconomical and ineffective, not so large as to be impersonal or unmanageable. We are almost completely self-contained, having our own premises, our own branches, other funeral directors from whom we have purchased our own pre-paid funeral plan, our own Memorial Garden Cremation Cemetery, our own small manufacturing plant, our own masonry connections, horses, carriage, a car fleet, you name it in the funeral industry; but most of all we have a most valuable and experienced staff whom it has taken years to bring together. They work together, sometimes play together and seem to share an incredible consideration for the business they are in.

It appears that everything is perfectly poised, so where do

we go from here? We are going to take some time to consolidate and 'enjoy the moment', as I like to say. This will give my sons a little more time to grow into their roles, something they are both doing admirably. I would like to finish off the Albin's Room in the Pump House Museum, Rotherhithe. I am very proud of this and enjoy working on it immensely; it will be something to leave for all time.

We are all looking forward to receiving our new fleet of cars, the development of which is keeping us very busy at the moment. Maybe we will open an extra branch – I know my sons would very much like to be involved with such a project. So if and when I think that the moment is right, I think I will put that in their hands. I am sure they will make a great job of it. Jon Fletcher and I are busy working on the Albin-Dyer Bermondsey and Rotherhithe Foundation charity and also helping the Evelina Children's Hospital appeal. More time too for writing, I hope. And perhaps for Jackie and me to have the odd trip to Italy and maybe spend some time on the water messing around with boats. Whatever happens, I will hang on to the reins for a bit longer, I think.

And the more distant future? More of the same if you please, but I am confident that my sons will pick up the historical mantle of F.A. Albin & Sons and, with each other's support – and mine too, I hope – enjoy every minute. I wish them all the best for their future. The future of Albin's itself will always be sincere and immeasurable. As for our grandchildren, who can tell what the long term will hold? As long as they are happy, that is all that matters. Olivia, aged just three, sometimes answers her home phone with 'F.A. Albin & Sons', and James, aged one, is so healthy and strong that maybe he will fulfil all our dreams and play football for England one day. With God's blessing, we still have Jonathan's future family to look forward to as well. I can't wait! I am sure that the future is sound and safe for F.A. Albin & Sons, especially for the Dyers.

Do I have any predictions for the future of funeral directing? Yes I do! I think that people are more than ever putting their faith in and realising the importance of the rituals surrounding a funeral and of going through them carefully. I hope that the true value of a funeral director who honestly dedicates his or her whole life to this honourable profession will be truly recognised in terms of the great deeds and great works that they do. My tip for the future is that the Swedish idea of freeze-drying (not to be confused with cryonics, of course, but if you have read my other two books you wouldn't be confused, would you?) might well become a common occurrence in the long term. It is environmentally friendly and a little more gentle than cremation, but with the same final effect. Time will tell, but remember – you heard it here first.

What about my funeral? What will it be like? Well, that's still for me to know and you to find out. Maybe I will write another book and tell you. One thing, however, that I would like to be sure of is that I will have some space just for me before then. The poet W.H. Davies wrote:

What is this life if, full of care,
We have no time to stand and stare?

But I think my old friend Winnie put it just as well when she recently advised me in a letter: 'Barry, find some time for yourself!'

POSTSCRIPT:
COME ON YOU BLUES, AND REDS, AND YELLOWS...

Sitting where I am today, looking back through my fifty-three years on this earth, I realise how important football has been to me and my life, perhaps the one pleasant distraction from my work that has always been safely there. It's a comforting hobby, and yet much more than that. If you are, first, a lover of football and, second, a lover of teams like I am, you will understand my affection for the following clubs and the people associated with them.

In Bermondsey, I was involved with three major clubs as a boy: CUM (Cambridge University Mission), OBC (Oxford and Bermondsey Club Stansfield) and Fisher Downside Worth. I spent time, through various stages of my childhood, at each of these clubs (with brief spells at a few others) – happy days with wonderful memories. The common denominator I enjoyed most of all was of course football, something that was vastly prominent in all three.

The Stansfield Club (OBC)

I spent many pleasant evenings and Saturday mornings on double-decker buses going to the Sports Federation ground for our football matches against other youth clubs, so have many happy childhood days to reflect on there. Today, the club is run, maintaining its proud traditions, by a remarkable group of people, too many to mention. They organise very successful boys clubs and very successful football teams full of Bermondsey lads and great characters. My admiration for this wonderful club and the people that surround it is endless. I always look for their football results and am very proud that they ask me to many of their events. They are amazing people and depict the character and the strengths of Bermondsey.

The club was founded by Dr John Stansfield, most widely known for founding the Oxford and Bermondsey Boys Club in 1897. The club was a precursor to modern-day youth projects and provided an alternative to the streets for boys and young men (what would nowadays be termed 'social inclusion'). Originally a civil servant, John Stansfield incredibly studied to become a doctor in his spare time. His vision has now gone from strength to strength, helping to fill many a Bermondsey teenager's spare time with constructive activities, sport and outings.

Home ground: The Boys Federation ground/St James/FKG.
Club colours: Usually blue and white (old Millwall kits from Roy Putt, ha ha).
Club song: The Club Hymn.
Finest player: Roy Putt (or so he tells me).
Best club man: Nobby – bless him he is great.
Best manager: Tumble (or so he tells me).

The Polytechnic Football Club

At the end of my school football days, I found it better to play my football outside Bermondsey, perhaps because it was important to keep some decorum while following my father and Fred into the business – the physical way in which I have always played the game might have detracted from my usual quiet conducting of funerals! Thanks to my sports teacher, Tim Ricks, I was able to go on a Business Studies course at the Polytechnic of Central London, now Westminster University. The Polytechnic Football Club ran ten sides at different levels, and its players came from all over the country. Some were students studying at the polytechnic, a vast array of talents – accountants, bank managers, lawyers, not many funeral directors though – but lots of everyday people like me. The polytechnic has been in my life since my fifteenth birthday and still plays a prominent part today. Friends and contacts, camaraderie, sportsmanship and the wonder of this club are ever present in my heart.

I have captained the first three sides at various stages of my life and have on odd occasions played for all ten sides (not all at once!), always for friendship and fun. It is perhaps more like an old-fashioned rugby club, where afterwards you would always buy a jug of beer and lemonade to make shandy up for the opposition. Whenever you were away, you received a meal; whenever at home, you served a meal for the opposition. The polytechnic certainly taught me a code of life that will stay with me always, and I owe many thanks to the polytechnic and the wonderful people who run and support it still.

The Polytechnic Football Club was founded in 1875 by Quintin Hogg, aided by fellow Old Etonian the Honourable A.F. Kinnaird (later to become Lord Kinnaird, President of the Football Association). It was named the Hanover Club, and its members met on Primrose Hill. On the neighbouring pitch played the team that later developed into Tottenham Hotspur FC. Other prominent members of the Polytechnic Club included J.F. Wall (later Sir Frederick Wall, the Football Association secretary) and Douglas M. Hogg (later the first Lord Hailsham). The late Lord Hailsham QC was (just like me!) a vice-president of the club.

During its long history, the club participated in many competitions, including the FA Cup, the Amateur Cup, Spartan League, Middlesex Senior League and cup competitions organised by the Amateur Football Alliance. Both my sons have also played here.

Ground: Polytechnic Stadium, Cavendish Road, Chiswick, W4.

Club colours: Originally red, green and black.

Club song: 'Polly Put the Kettle on' – just for fun!

Finest player: No not me – there are so many that I cannot choose, and they are all my pals anyway. Maybe Jeff Lloyd, my striking partner in the first team, but Tim and Ted Ricks are my heroes.

Best club man: John Kean – amazing fellow.

Best manager: Hugh Linsey/Dave Christmas. (Not me, although I'm still their best funeral director!)

Fisher Athletic Football Club (affiliated in its early days with Downside and Worth and Fisher)

Right on my doorstep downtown in the Surrey Docks Stadium, this club is full of lovely people, real football supporters young and old. This was one of the first cell-net pitches in the country, which drains and holds water for use on dry days, unique considering it was built so long ago now. Both my sons have played for Fisher Athletic, and I have spent many happy days there as President and now Life President of the club. The club is currently negotiating the purchase of the land and a rebuilding of the stadium so that football will go on for ever at Surrey Docks. We hope the future will hold a new football academy there too, to continue the club's triumphant history.

The original Fisher Club was founded in 1908 by the John Fisher Catholic Society, whose aim was to provide football facilities for underprivileged children in the London district of Bermondsey. However, this team folded in 1964. Fisher Athletic was then reformed two years later, playing in the Kent Amateur League before joining the London Spartan League in 1974. At this point, the club played on a poorly equipped pitch at Mitcham in Surrey, and their main achievements had been winning the London Intermediate Cup in 1959/60 and the Surrey Intermediate Cup in 1961/62. They were always keen though to return to their base in London's Docklands, and in 1982 Fisher were able to relocate to their current Surrey Docks Stadium. In the same season, they won the Spartan League championship for the second successive season, and their new facilities enabled them to join the Southern League.

Fisher won the Southern League Southern Division title at the first attempt with 23 wins from their 34 games. Among their star players were skipper Dennis Sharp, who made over 750 appearances for the club and later had a spell as manager; top scorer and 205 goal club record marksman Paul Shinners, who joined Gillingham in 1984; his brother Bobby; and Dave Samson, brother of England full back

Kenny. They were also Merit Cup winners as the league's top-scoring side. In 1983/84, Fisher were narrowly pipped to the Premier Division title by Dartford, but after lifting the Southern League Cup in 1984/85 they won the league championship in 1986/87. The club was led to this success by ambitious chairman Terry McCarthy and Manager Dogan Arif. Among the stars of this side were leading goal scorer Trevor Dark, goal keeper David Fry, Chris Lewington, Ray Shinners (brother of Paul and Bobby), Ricky Hodgson, Alan Hodges, Burt Davies, Paul Collins and Chris Hiscock (Scruff).

During the 1980s, the club won the London Senior Cup three times and the Kent Senior Cup once, as well as reaching the FA Cup First Round Proper twice, losing to Bristol City in 1984/85 and Bristol Rovers in 1987/88. In 1987/88, Fisher took their place in the Southern Division but were relegated back to the Southern League in 1991 and a year later finished second from bottom of the Premier Division. Since then, the club has played in the Southern Division, although following a spell of managerial uncertainty last season, all is now well and looking good for the future, thanks to new chairman Sami Mudd.

Home ground: Surrey Docks Stadium, Salter Road, SE16.
Club colours: Black and white stripes.
Club song: 'Come on the Fish' and 'Downtown'.
Finest player: Again an endless choice, but Dave Mehmett has it for me.
Best club man: Charlie Bennett, Les Rowe, Jimmy Titchener, John O'Grady, Johnny Burke and many more.
Best manager: Dogan Arif (who would dare dispute that? – not me – but I truly admire his leadership).

Millwall Football Club

The old Den was the first ground I ever visited to see a football match: as a young boy, I went along with a few pals slightly older than me from Tranton Road. Millwall were very much in the low divisions in those days, but it was great fun. Programmes, Percy Dalton's peanuts, hot dogs, rattles, rosettes, scarves and bobble hats (just like Chris and Andy wear at Chelsea), wonderful memories and wonderful days. It was honestly a great pleasure to go and see football played with spirit, camaraderie and real guts. The supporters sing 'No one likes us', but I don't know why; they are not a bad lot, I can vouch for that. I have been on the terraces at both the old Den and the new Den, sat in the directors' box, received corporate hospitality and had a box of my own. Whenever possible, I go with my sons to the games. Milwall is wonderful club with a wonderful history built around working-class areas and working-class people. I personally really feel at home here.

Millwall FC was formed in 1885 by the workers of the J.T. Morton jam and marmalade factory in the West Ferry Road on the Isle of Dogs. Nearly all of the workers were Scottish immigrants and therefore adopted the rampant lion of their home flag. The football club that they set up was to be called Millwall Rovers. Their first ever fixture was on 3rd October 1885, against Fillebrook who played at Leyton. The new team were thrashed 5–0.

In November 1886, the East End Football Association was formed, and with it came a senior cup competition. Millwall made it to the final against London Caledonians, the game being played at the Leyton Cricket Ground. The match ended 2–2, and the teams shared the trophy for six months each.

Despite an 8–1 drubbing in the FA Cup (then known as the English Cup), Millwall recovered well and kept the trophy as their property. Not bad for a side that was still in its infancy! Millwall went on to become founder members of the Southern League, which they won for the first two years of its existence. In those days, the Football League was still in the early days in its development and consisted mainly of northern clubs such as Bury, Notts County, Sheffield United and Preston North End. In the south, the Southern League was not only seen as a rival but as equally prestigious.

Millwall played on a variety of sites on the Isle of Dogs, becoming known as 'The Dockers' by the inhabitants of the Island. It was not unusual for Millwall to attract thirty or even forty thousand spectators to a game, especially at their second ground in North Ferry Road, which was quite an achievement given that the travelling facilities were sparse. Their most famous ground though was the Den at New Cross, into which they moved in 1910. The first ever match there was against Brighton & Hove Albion (who spoiled the celebrations by winning from the only goal!). It was here that the famous 'roar' was developed. The Den soon became one of the most feared grounds in the country: no team liked to play there as the crowd and the place itself created an intimidating atmosphere. Milwall became known as a hard cup-fighting team, and there were memorable matches against Derby County, Sunderland and others that saw packed crowds of over forty thousand at the Den in the 1930s and '40s.

In 1944/45, Millwall appeared in a Southern FA Cup Final at Wembley against Chelsea, but because it was an 'unofficial' wartime cup final, this is not even acknowledged in the record books. With the loss of so many young men, including footballers, during the war, it was difficult for all the

214

clubs to retain their former status. This was especially true for Millwall, who appeared to suffer more than most. From being one of the country's biggest clubs before the war, Millwall were reduced to being one of its smallest afterwards. Their form during the 1950s was poor, and they suffered relegation on a regular basis. It was not until the early '60s that things began to change. During this time, they 'discovered' a number of useful players, goalkeeper Alec Stepney being one. He later went on to fame with Manchester United, winning a European Cup Winners Medal in 1968.

Later in the decade, Millwall established an incredible record of fifty-nine home matches without defeat, largely thanks to Manager Ron Gray, who laid the foundations, and Benny Fenton, who continued to build on Gray's side. In the early 1970s, Millwall boasted a truly great side, now remembered by Lions fans as 'The Class of '71'. This was a team that boasted the inspirational Harry Cripps, Derek Posse, Barry Kitchener, Keith Weller, Doug Allder and more. They lost out on promotion by just one point.

What goes up must come down, so they say, and after the highs of the early 70s, Millwall seemed to hit the lows again. It was then that ex-Arsenal player George Graham took control and transformed both club and team. Promotion to Division 2 was followed by a financial crisis that nearly saw the club go under. However, in 1985 a new company was formed to save the club from extinction.

George Graham had done a grand job but felt the need to move on. He was replaced by John Docherty, who had a poor first season but then broke the spell and took Millwall to Division 1 as champions the following year. Everyone of course predicted that Millwall would drop straight back down, but by October 1988 Millwall were top of Division 1.

Up front, the Lions boasted a deadly strike force of Teddy Sheringham and Tony Cascarino. Both would leave the club in time, but while at the Den both gave total commitment. Teddy Sheringham, although now a free agent, is still a regular visitor to Millwall home games. Millwall has become including well known as a breeding ground for young talent, as well as Teddy Sheringham, Alec Stepney, Keith Weller, Steve Lovell, John Fashanu, Tony Cascarino, Gordon Hill, Eamon Dunphy, Ben Thatcher, Neil Emblem, Phil Babb, Neil Ruddock, John McGinlay, Keith Branagan, Kasey Keller, Andy Roberts, John Cunningham . . . all these and more began their football careers at the Den.

Millwall fans are genuine, extremely passionate and will give all for their Lions. But they expect the players to return the compliment and give 100% to the cause.

Home ground: The Den
Club colours: Blue and white.
Club song: 'Let 'em Come, let 'em Come, let 'em All Come Down to the Den.'
Finest player: So many, but I guess Len Julians, Barry Rowan and Alec Stepney.
Best club man: Roy Putt – kit man (or so he tells me).
Best manager: Wisey and Wilkins, of course, but also many before.

Liverpool Football Club

Liverpool is also a club richly steeped in history built around working-class people and a dockland area, not dissimilar to that of Millwall, not quite as old but many more trophies! I came to love and admire Liverpool through the late 1960s and onwards. Bill Shankly is my all-time footballing hero, and, even today, when I see old films of him speaking, I get a shiver up my back; what a great leader. Although Liverpool were perhaps first brought to me through the power of television, they are a club I have visited many times. I have truly enjoyed the passion, emotion and atmosphere that surround Anfield, perhaps the finest ground I have ever been to. You see, I really am a football fan first, foremost and last. I love Liverpool, and so do my boys.

The history of Liverpool Football Club is an incredibly rich one: a truly comprehensive history would run to many volumes. My concise history can really only trace the major developments in the club's fortunes.

In 1888, the Football League kicked off for the first time, and at Anfield, Everton, the city of Liverpool's biggest club of the day, were the home side. John Houlding, brewer of 'sparkling ales', a mover and shaker in Liverpool politics and a good part of the brains and money behind Everton Football Club, was at that time the owner of the Anfield Road ground. In 1892, however, Everton parted company with Houlding over the issue of rent paid on the ground. Houlding was left with a ground but no team – but not for long. He was fortunate that talented Irishman John McKenna, a member of the Everton coaching staff, stayed loyal to him. With a hefty loan (for those days) of £500, McKenna set about building Liverpool Football Club.

McKenna looked for talent and assembled a team that became known as the 'team of the Macs'. With the exception of goalkeeper and Englishman Bill McOwen, the team all hailed from Scotland. After a modest double in their first season when they took the Lancashire League title and the Liverpool District Cup, Liverpool entered the new Football

League Second Division. But something was happening at Anfield . . . gates rose from a few hundred to over three thousand once word got around about the side's high scoring habits.

Sadly, though, the runaway success came to an end, and the newly promoted team crashed out of the First Division at the end of the season. However, they then bounced back in fine style, taking the Second Division by storm to return to the First Division, determined to stay there. After finishing as FA Cup runners-up in 1899, Liverpool captured the League Championship in 1901 under the guidance of McKenna's canny successor, Tom Watson. The Anfield Club had arrived among the teams to be reckoned with. The year 1901 was no fluke, the title returning to Anfield again in 1906. But the now established side needed more room for its growing army of fans. And the rest, as they say, is history and probably known to every football fan! The '70s, '80s and '90s have been just legendary.

Home ground: Anfield.
Club colours: Red.
Club song: 'You'll Never Walk Alone.'
Finest player: Dalgleish, Keegan, Owen, Rush . . so many!
Best club man: All those in the legendary boot room.
Best manager: Bill Shankly.

Football 2004

So I have the Stansfield Club from my childhood playing days, the Polytechnic Football Club where I played most of my football, the Fisher Club where I enjoyed my sons playing so much. Millwall, the club I followed as a boy, I still follow today, Bermondsey through and through. Liverpool has a place in my heart and a passion I can only admire. When people talk about the greatest players of all time and players they have admired so much, the Bests, the Peles, the Maradonnas, the Cruyffs, although I too have enjoyed watching them, I, like everybody else, have my own special player. My idol as a younger man was always Peter Osgood, the wizard of Stansford Bridge, playing in that wonderful side with Tommy Doherty as manager, alongside Hutchinson, Hudson, McCready, Harris, Cook, Baldwin, Boyle . . . the list goes on and on.

I was very much an admirer of the Chelsea team of that era, and followed these games weekly, but perhaps the greatest fun of all has come from watching my sons play football, something I still do every Sunday. It has been a real salvation to the end of my playing days watching them, and I would advise everyone to do this if you get the chance. It is second only to playing yourself – which these days is not as frequent. I can still help, and still be wheeled out from time to time for the odd charity game, and long may it continue.

Millwall for the Cup (well, almost!)

22 May 2004 – a day that will forever live in the hearts of Bermondsey, Rotherhithe, Southwark and Lewisham. You see, it is not often that we in Bermondsey are given a chance to show our solidarity, our personality and our love for football and the area itself, so imagine the local passion that was waiting to expose itself through the blue and white colours of Millwall FC. We were, as always, the underdogs, but this time we were for real in the FA Cup final at the Millennium Stadium in Cardiff. It seemed like nothing this good had ever

happened to us before. We were actually there. Sure, we might have had the luck of the draw and scraped through a couple of games, but we were there. Over six hundred clubs entered the FA Cup and we were one of the last two left in the competition, along with a little-known club called Manchester United (surely just a small hurdle to climb – well, we are entitled to dream just the same as anyone else).

Television crews interviewing local people from the Blue invaded Bermondsey. Even the club chaplain, Reverend Owen Beamont OBE, a very good friend of mine, was interviewed. He also made a very interesting point when he said, 'Our Blessed Lady also wore blue and white.' Sounds like a good omen then – what do you think?

For once, we ordinary people in Bermondsey were in the limelight, sucked in with the magic of the Cup and its romance. The local council invested in banners saying 'Millwall good luck for the Cup'. As they went up, I remember thinking, 'They will be good souvenirs – they won't stay there for long.' Sure enough they didn't, and I noticed in our local paper a comment from the editor: 'Southwark Council is pleading please don't steal our banners, we want to make Southwark special for the 22nd May, please put them back' (no chance there, mate). Bermondsey was awash with blue and white bunting, flags hanging from every window, every car tooting its horn and flying flags of St George and 'Millwall for the Cup'. Local pubs had huge banners hanging from their windows and rooftops. Quite rightly, we were milking it for everything we had.

I secured our tickets on the first day they came on sale. Sadly, my elder son Simon was off on his holidays and could do nothing about it, but Jonathan, his wife-to-be Jane, our mechanic Kenny, my great friend Ricky, young Ernie Cooksey, a great friend of the family who now plays for Oldham Athletic, and Paul from work, who is one of the greatest Millwall fans I have ever met, stocked up with good grub, lots of sweets and crisps, and climbed into our Kia people-carrier to join the thousands of other local fans on the way to Cardiff.

Jonathan had rigged up a DVD player so we could watch DVDs if we got stuck in traffic on the way home, and he had put two Millwall flags streaming from the windows of the driver's and passenger doors. I took the first stint of driving to pick up Ricky and was only a few miles up the road when I felt the need for a little fresh air and lowered the front window, only to watch the flag, eventually like our dreams, fly off into infinity. After a volley of abuse from everybody in the vehicle, we decided it might be a good omen – one flag missing, one nil. You hang on to anything when you are the underdog.

We decided to drive straight to Newport, park the car and get the train for the short fifteen-minute journey to Cardiff, which proved to be very successful. This would put us at least six junctions down the M4 coming home and give us the opportunity to miss most of the traffic. As we arrived at the stadium, I was moved to a few tears as I saw so many faces I knew and the streams of blue and white, and heard the cries of 'No one like us!' It was a beautiful moment.

The crowds were really not segregated in any way so we were able to mingle, many fans having discussions about the game to come. Light banter but no trouble, and that quite truly gave me the greatest feeling of all. I was very proud of where I came from, proud of my roots. There was the odd person the worse for wear sitting in a corner sleeping it off but they were few and far between. Most people were just full of life and having a great day.

We got into the stadium as early as we could, around about

221

half past one, just to soak up the atmosphere. The first thing that struck me as I looked around was that the blue and white of the Millwall end and side were already saturated with people not wishing to miss a moment. The Manchester United area was practically empty, maybe to say, 'Well, we've been here so often this is nothing new to us,' but we didn't care. We were there and singing and enjoying ourselves and having a wonderful time.

My old friend Roy Putt, the kit man, walked out on to the pitch full of pride and with tears in his eyes. Coming towards us, he gave us a wave and pointed out some of his family so that I could say hi to them. Jonathan's friend and neighbour Tim Cahill (a Millwall mid-fielder) came out for a warm-up but Jonathan could not attract his attention! Jonathan was, I know, very proud to know Tim and would, I was sure, have plenty of conversations about the day with him over the coming weeks.

One of my pet hates, I have to tell you, is anything bumping into my glasses, dislodging them, affecting their comfort in any way or knocking them off, so to that end I was very conscious of all the light beach balls and wind floaters milling around the stadium. I thought to myself, 'I'll be forever conscious of one of them hitting me in a moment.' Sure enough, at the magic moment that the teams were announced, the biggest one of all hit me smack in the nose, knocking my glasses down my face and dislodging the little plastic noseguards. I turned to Jonathan and Jane, and said, 'Oh quickly, I've lost the plastic piece for my glasses.' Scouring the floor, we could not see it anywhere, and the teams were about to come on to the field. Thankfully, as Jane stood up she noticed that it was still stuck to my nose! And this at the most crucial moment.

Jonathan took the piece to repair it but, you've guessed it, he dropped it again, and there we were, back on the floor, asking everyone to move their feet so we could find it. Luckily we did find it, and Jane took over to replace it quickly. I could not even do this myself as I could not see anything clearly. Just at the vital moment, I was able to get my glasses back on so I missed nothing. The lovely FA Cup hymn 'Abide with Me' and our National Anthem were sung to perfection, with respect shown from both sides. We were easily outsinging the Manchester United fans, and that went on throughout the game, filling me with great pride.

We defended well throughout the game, and in reality we did not attack at all. Many will say that we played a negative game and could have been a bit more ambitious. That's certainly a fair point: I would have changed things a little more quickly and taken a more attacking view, but the reality of it all was that no matter what we did with the team, we were not going to win that day. Manchester United's class was evident for all to see. We had some crucial injuries and, unlike Manchester United, did not have the strength or depth in our squad to cope with that. In reality, we had to play a number of youngsters, which is great for the future but left us very short of experience. The final score was of course 3–0 to Manchester United (perhaps a little flattering, as I am sure that Van Nistlerooy was offside for his second goal), but on the day the best team won.

Also on the day, the lesser supporters were the greater ones. We won at the singing and were clearly the noisier of the two camps of supporters in every way. Then it occurred to me that teams will come and go – there will be better Millwall teams and worse ones in years to come – but the supporters are there for ever, and on that day, 22 May 2004, the Millwall supporters proved a very special point. Millwall's old bad reputation was cast aside, and we showed the world that we are good people who know our football, are full of pride and come from a very special part of the world – Bermondsey. Even if our ground does happen to fall in the boundaries of the Lewisham Borough, we are the all-round winners. For me, that battle had been won, and we left for home with that firmly in our hearts.

During the game, Paul had had the great fortune to catch the match ball as it flew into the crowd. He held it firmly in his arms for about five seconds so that no one could grab it and allowed me just to touch the ball as he threw it back on to the pitch, a moment we will never forget. We had the FA Cup ball in our hands – what fun.

When we left the ground, the two sets of supporters were mingling together. There was no trouble, no trouble at all. A few Manchester fans even recognised me from *Don't Drop the Coffin*, which was fun, and I felt I was among good people all day long. As we got off the train in Newport and into our car for the journey home, we sat listening to Talk Sport Radio. It crossed my mind how I had been asked the week before whether I wanted to join in the recording of the Millwall song. Unfortunately I was unable to do this, but my good friend Phil Burkett, a real Bermondsey boy, will never know how lucky he was that I could not turn up that day because I have to admit that I do not have the best of voices. I chuckled to myself. Memories are a beautiful place from which we can never be removed, and this day had been a memory I would take to the grave with me.

Bermondsey had been deserted that Saturday. Nobody was outside, nobody was shopping, anyone left behind without a ticket was in some pub or other watching the football or at home in front of the telly with friends. On the Sunday, 23 May, all Bermondsey turned out in the Blue, Southwark Park Road, to watch its team do a lap of Bermondsey in honour. The supporters were singing 'Millwall's European Tour', reflecting the fact that we will be playing in Europe next year.

There you go, never mind the new camp Barcelona, the new Den Millwall is where I would like to be in charge of the incoming travel, so I could greet the coaches and take them all round Bermondsey. You would see the Real Madrid or Barcelona team going round Bermondsey thinking, 'Where am I? Who the hell are we playing?' Well, you will soon find out, lads. We are going to strengthen the team for next year and have a lot of fun in Europe.

One of the most wonderful memories of the day I will cherish was the emotion shown by a local family who lost their husband and father, John, just before this. So passionate a Millwall fan was John that his family had him home in the front room so they could watch the Cup Final with him before his funeral on the following Monday. A moving gesture of love that I will never forget and which just sums us up – we were all one!

So an ode to our local pubs, who housed so many of us to watch the match:

They're knocking down our local pub – **boo**
But they're building a new one – **hurrah**
There's only one bar – **boo**
But it's a mile long – **hurrah**
They don't sell beer – **boo**
They give it away – **hurrah**
There's only one barmaid – **boo**
To every customer – **hurrah**

> Millwall didn't win the Cup – **boo**
> But they got there anyway – **hurrah**

Well done Theo, Dennis, Ray, the players, the coaching team.
Well done Millwall. Well done you supporters, and well done
South London. And thanks for the memory Millwall, a great
day!